God Exists

Evidence of Biblical Miracles Brought to Light

God Exists

Evidence of Biblical Miracles Brought to Light

Sylke Claridge

God Exists

Evidence of Biblical Miracles Brought to Light

© Sylke Claridge 2024

All rights reserved. Without limiting the rights under copyright reserved above, no part of this publication may be reproduced, stored in a retrieval system, or transmitted, in any form or by any means (electronic, mechanical, photocopying, recording or otherwise), without the prior written permission of the copyright owner of this book.

Published by
Lighthouse Christian Publishing
SAN 257-4330
228 Freedom Parkway
Hoschton, GA 30548
United States of America

www.lighthousechristianpublishing.com

For Alex

I give heartfelt thanks to Suzi Alessandra for first proofreading, to Sue Prytherch and Eilish Bouchier for their constructive criticism.

And to Andy Overett, my publisher, for taking a chance on me.

Sylke Claridge

Miracles and God

Testimony and Evidence
of Miracles which happened a long time ago

For my Father in Heaven and The Children of this World who want to believe in God

And a Big Thank you to all the Heroes of this book who worked and found the evidence – I am just the collector of all.

Preface

Have you ever read by yourself one whole page of the book called the Bible? If yes, did you ask yourself if anything in the Bible written is true, and relevant to today's age? Did you ever wonder if there was any archaeological or geological evidence left from miracles and stories told in the Bible, proof to be shown today that God's signs and wonders really happened?

Did you ever ask yourself if God exists? And Jesus, his son? Then this booklet is for you. As a child I believed whole heartedly in God. I was given a Children's Bible to read which I found so much easier to digest than the Bible. My mum taught me the loveliest prayer for a child. It goes like this: "Lieber Gott, mach mich fromm, dass ich in den Himmel komm" A rough translation is:

"Dear Father mine, make me devout, so that Heaven will be proud."

Later I still believed and prayed as a Christian but also thought that all other religions have a valid core and everywhere good people are to be found; the latter I still find to be true. Then I went on a quest to find truth in history and politics – and the more evil and deception became evident to me, the more I prayed and turned to God and finally started to read the book of God, the Bible, from A to Z, previously only having heard the same sermons all over again presented in different churches, different countries. My partner at the time had viewed the videos of Rob Skiba and Rob's explanation of the Fallen Angels and Nephilim and the following generations of giants. Fascinating stuff! Giants of all different heights existed! Shortly afterwards I stumbled over Ron Wyatt's archaeological discoveries. My curiosity was fanned wondering if all written in the Bible is fact and not fiction or mythology as presented today and if more evidence could be presented to support that the word of God is unquestionably true. These findings I want to showcase here in this little booklet.

Mark Twain said: " The two most important days in your life are the day you are born and the day you find out why." Let's see if God and the Bible can help you to find out why you were born. I now believe that the end of times according to the Book of Revelation is near and all will be revealed when God determines to do so and Jesus will return one day; hopefully that day will be soon.

Which meaning does the Bible have today for you, dear reader? What is the Bible? Myth, Allegory or Fact? The word of God? The Bible is a book of faithful people and sinners in extraordinary circumstances, either cursed or helped in their actions by supernatural events; it is a history book of God's people and their enemies, of Kings and ordinary people who lived a long time ago, their actions and deeds remembered through the Holy Spirit and literally, I believe, dictated to the authors, the first one Moses who penned down the book of Genesis, our creation. It is a book of armies fighting and a victory gained by purely marching and sound. The walls of Jericho fell after the Israelites marched around the city walls once a day for six days, seven times on the seventh day, and then blew their trumpets. Sound, frequency and intent are energy and science is discovering that frequency can be used for healing or destruction, but only with the power of God the Israelites gained their victory (Joshua 6:NIV New International Version).

It is commonly argued that a third of the Bible is prophecy, a third is poetry and a third is history.

Prophecy is the foretelling of the future. And who would know better than God what the future holds? It is a book that tells of the second coming of God's son and him reigning supreme, a good King, his name is Jesus.

The Bible is a book that comforts us of a Father, who is loving and merciful if you adhere to his commandments and who promises you an eternal life in Heaven. This Father is merciful to the extent that he demanded for cities to be set aside to be refuge havens for murderers who killed without intent.

Numbers 35:6 NIV (New International Version, there are several official English translations in circulation, I cite mostly this NIV and the KJV, King James Version)

'Six of the towns you give to the Levites will be cities of refuge, to which a person who has killed someone may flee. In addition, give them forty-two other towns.'

It is a good passage to read as God distinguishes between accidental and unintended homicide and the accidental murderer doesn't forfeit his future life in a prison, amazing justice.

And later God was so merciful that he sent his Son down from Heaven to be beaten and crucified to atone for our sins despite never having harmed a living soul. What could I possibly add to the Bible, the most read book on earth through the centuries? It is estimated to have sold over 40 Million copies in the last sixty years only. I am trying to showcase all the geological evidence of the miracles God performed here on earth and furnish a stepping-stone as to how to build up faith. It is surprising to me that it is not openly taught at school, in Universities and Churches – to me it is fact that every miracle and event described in the Bible really happened and should be part of our history. And I wish with my heart and soul that some of what I am writing about will fan your curiosity, pierce your heart or whatever needs to be touched, to research yourself and see if there is a grain of truth in all of this.

Of course, if you already do believe in Jesus and his almighty Father, then you might know all you are about to read. Maybe you want to plod on, maybe there is still some knowledge hidden here which you didn't possess? God says about attaining wisdom in Proverbs 4:6-7

"Do not forsake wisdom, and she will protect you; love her, and she will watch over you. Wisdom is supreme; therefore get wisdom. Though it costs all you have, get understanding."

All artwork is done by approximation – if you want to see photos please search the net, all was still readily visible when I wrote this. I only included photos when I felt compelled to do so and photo-shopped them not to infringe on any copyright except all images over 70 years old, which belong to the public domain. So far I did not find any evidence for the existence of the Garden Eden. 😊

So my story starts with Noah's Ark. Why did God order Noah to build the Ark? Has the Ark been found somewhere here on this earth? Actually -The first story you need to understand is of fallen Angels and Giants because these beings here on earth transgressed God's commands and therefore he caused the flood! What does the Bible reveal about them?

The Fallen Angels and Giants

Genesis 6:1-3 (Holy Bible, printed by James McKay, Sydney, 1873)

And it came to pass, when men began to multiply on the face of the earth, and daughters were born unto them, that the sons of God saw the daughters of men that they were fair; and they took them wives of all which they chose.

And the Lord said, My Spirit shall not always strive with man, for that he also is flesh: yet his days shall be a hundred and twenty years.

The Sons of God? Who were these sons? It all sounds far-fetched but please bear with me.

To compare: Genesis 6:1-3 NIV

When men began to increase in number on earth and daughters were born to them, the sons of God saw that the daughters of men were beautiful, and they married any of them they chose. Then the Lord said,

"My spirit will not contend with man forever, for he is mortal; his days will be a hundred and twenty years."

Did you know that God had sons? His angels are his sons and daughters in Heaven and some of them were sent to earth to help newly created mankind with tools and living, even how to make music. This one can read in the Book of Enoch.

These angels were lusting after the beautiful maidens of earth or they wanted to gain power on earth....By the way, up until then men and women could live to an old age of over 900 years. Methuselah, the great grandfather of Noah, lived until he was 969 years old. But that was before the flood. (Genesis 5:31 NIV)

And Genesis 6:4 (Holy Bible, printed by James McKay, Sydney, 1873)

There were giants in the earth in those days; and also after that, when the sons of God came in unto the daughters of men, and they bore children to them; the same became mighty men, which were of old, men of renown.

To compare: Genesis 6:4 NIV

The Nephilim were on the earth in those days – and also afterward - when the sons of God went to the daughters of men and had children by them. They were the heroes of old, men of renown.

Very confusing. So God sent his Angels down to earth to help mankind and they were very good looking and powerful otherworldly beings, winged or not, and they took beautiful women to be their wives. And as these beings were now the dominant race here on earth, they did whatever they pleased. The only mishap not according to their plan was the following: The offspring born to the women they cohabited with were growing tall or very tall.

And this could have happened here on this Earth? You may have watched movies of Thor and the Titans and believe it to be fiction. But today more and more evidence is emerging that giants were living on this earth. There were very big giants before the flood and smaller ones after the flood. Rob Skiba produced a few good videos named the Archeon Invasion about them.

Who were these giants or Nephilim? Did you ever hear of them? If you are into Computer Games then you might have encountered them as a 40K Nephilim. According to the Lexicanum for players "The Nephilim were a minor but malevolent xenos species encountered on Melchior by the Blood Angels and the Luna Wolves during the Great Crusade. They fed on adoration and worship and subjugated their world's native population in order to satisfy this hunger." Pretty much accurate according to Genesis in the Bible and the Apocrypha (more about this later) and how is it that a game designer knows so much about them?

Wikipedia has a bit less to divulge about them:

'The Nephilim are mysterious beings or people in the Hebrew Bible who are described as being large and strong.'

The Book of Enoch also speaks of these Nephilim and explains what they are in detail. This Book has been part of the Ethiopian Bible at the time when Jesus was walking this earth; the Ethiopian Bible has 88 books still today and one must wonder why the Roman Emperor Constantine has taken out 22 books at the council of Nicaea in AD 325. These 22 books are named or shamed Apocrypha for the Western canon, which means they are not considered canonically or historically true, but they are contained in the Ethiopic Bible, and older Bibles from the last century may still have some apocryphal books included as does my old Holy Bible by James McKay, Sydney, 1873.

The Book of Enoch was widely known by early Christians until the fourth century AD, when it was banned by the Church authorities and virtually disappeared. It describes how Enoch walked with the Archangels who took him up to Heaven and revealed to him the secrets of the universe and the future of mankind. This book was rediscovered in 1773 in Ethiopia (where it always was) and first translated into English in 1820, ten years later into German. According to most scholars, part of it was written in the third century BCE and other parts in the first century CE. Different historians have different opinions about the age of the manuscript.

And then there are the Dead Sea Scrolls, which have been unearthed in 1947 in tatters and scrolls by some shepherds in long forgotten caves in Israel. What could be deciphered has now been reprinted- it is the best reading beside the Book of Enoch as it explains in detail how the world became corrupted and evil before the flood.

Back to the rebellious group of Angels: The Book of Enoch testifies that the sons of God were 200 Angels who rebelled against the word of God and married the beautiful daughters of the earth. What happened exactly is written in Enoch 7 (Section II) Missing Books of the Bible: It's a bigger story than any Superman movie, still almost no feature film has been produced, imbibe it as it would have really happened because it has happened.

1 It happened after the sons of men had multiplied in those days, that daughters were born to them, elegant and beautiful.

2 And when the angels, the sons of heaven, beheld them, they became enamored of them, saying to each other, Come, let us select for ourselves wives from the progeny of men, and let us beget children.

3 Then their leader Samyaza said to them; I fear that you may perhaps be indisposed to the performance of this enterprise;

4 And that I alone shall suffer for so grievous a crime.

5 But they answered to him and said; We all swear;

6 And bind ourselves by mutual execrations, that we will not change our intention, but execute our projected undertaking.

7 Then they swore all together, and all bound themselves by mutual execrations. Their whole number was two hundred, who descended upon Ardis, which is the top of mount Armon.

9 These are the names of their chiefs: Samyaza, who was their leader, Urakabarameel, Akibeel, Tamiel, Ramuel, Danel, Azkeel, Saraknyal, Asael, Armers, Batraal, Anane, Zavebe, Samsaveel, Ertael, Turel, Yomiyael, Arazyal. These were the prefects of the two hundred angels, and the remainder were all with them.

10 Then they took wives, each choosing for himself, whom they began to approach, and with them they cohabited; teaching them sorcery, incantations, and the dividing of roots and trees.

11 And the women conceived and brought forth giants,

12 Whose stature was each three hundred cubits. These devoured all which the labor of men produced; until it became impossible to feed them; 300 Cubits!

Did you read this? How tall is that? The Sky Tower in Bucharest, Romania, created by Viennese architectural firm Hoffman-Janz Architekten ZT Gmbh has exactly a height of 137 meters. It is Romania's tallest building and has 42 stories. We can hardly fathom that people of that stature existed, or can you?

13 When they turned themselves against men, in order to devour them;

14 And began to injure birds, beasts, reptiles, and fishes, to eat their flesh one after another, and to drink their blood.

15 Then the earth reproved the unrighteous.

Enoch 8

1 Moreover Azazyel taught men to make swords, knives, shields, breastplates, the fabrication of mirrors, and the workmanship of bracelets and ornaments, the use of paint, the beautifying of eyebrows, the use of stones of every valuable and select kind, and all sorts of dyes, so that the world became altered.

(Interesting to observe that these skills obviously are in existence in Heaven and not all of them are bad if you know how to operate them with a good intent and good heart –But here on earth where God is testing you, we should not try to predict the future via astrology without having God in our hearts first. God as our father can give you prophetic dreams and much more – but without him we might be under the umbrella of evil because the Prince of Darkness is in charge, a bit like the 'Hunger Games')

Enoch 8 continued

2 Impiety increased; fornication multiplied; and they transgressed and corrupted all their ways.

3 Amazarak taught all the sorcerers, and dividers of roots;

4 Armers taught the solution of sorcery;

5 Barkayal taught the observers of the stars;

6 Akibeel taught signs;

7 Tarmiel taught astronomy;

8 And Asaradel taught the motion of the moon.

The Nephilim or Fallen Angels were either sent by God to teach mankind these skills and arts and turned rebellious on earth, when they lusted after the beautiful women here; or they dissented first and then came to earth to gain power and the women, and of course part of their power was a supernatural one stemming from Heaven. If you have a look at ancient Sumerian tablets, you find depictions of angel-winged beings, some of them with a head of a hawk or a fishtail back. Common sense would deduce that these beings were real, not imagined, supernatural and therefore not of God's creation of mankind. These were the so-called Fallen Angels and they took women for their wives and created very big giants. About that God says: you have gained not the real wisdom of heaven but just the magic arts.

ENOCH Chapter 16:3

"You have been in Heaven, but all the mysteries had not yet been revealed to you, and you knew worthless ones, and these in the hardness of your hearts you have made known to women, and through these mysteries women and men work much evil on earth."

They knew that they were acting against the word of God and therefore united and formed a pact to not abandon each other. Please consider that even in Heaven there is free will and also dissent. Later, when they saw how much wrong they had done, they petitioned Enoch to intercede for them and gain mercy. Enoch was a very devout and special man, dedicated to the Lord and so pious that God took him to Heaven during his life and then sent him back to Earth. To think that in that time you could have had a conversation with a man who experienced Heaven. Read the book of Enoch, it is fascinating and describes in detail how the luminaries traverse the earth.

So, Enoch could space-travel between Heaven and Earth; he also never died but was taken to Heaven.

Genesis 5:21-24 NIV

When Enoch lived 65 years he became the father of Methuselah. After he became the father of Methuselah, Enoch walked with God for 300 years and had other sons and daughters. Altogether Enoch lived 365 years. Enoch walked with God, then he was no more, because God took him away.

God did decline Enoch's petition because these Angels produced much havoc on earth. The seed of these renegade Angels was so strong that the children being born were growing up to be giants as you have read before. And no, that doesn't mean that they all exploded their mum's bellies as they could have been born at normal size and then grew to a big height. But maybe the text below describes what really happened?

-The Book of Enoch
-Ethopic text.

~And the daughters of Cain with whom the angels had companied conceived, but they were unable to bring forth their children, and they died. And of the children who were in their wombs some died, and some came forth having split open the bellies of their mothers they came forth by their navels. And when they were grown up and reached man's estate they became giants, whose height reached unto the clouds.

These giants might have been helpful creating huge buildings and working with big stones and this would solve the mystery of the pyramids or other megalithic structures – lots of them now under water after the flood, but they also needed a fair amount of food and when the land did not produce enough to eat it seems that the giants started to devour the inhabitants of this earth. Very scary to imagine that time. And it seems that these Angels and their offspring the Nephilim also did some gene splicing and breeding Chimeras, human-animal hybrids like the Minotaur or other mixed species. God did not like that anyone tampered with his creation – would you?

God actually explicitly forbids mixing species in Leviticus 19:19 NIV

"Keep my decrees. **Do not mate with different kinds of animals.**"

There are stories all around Earth about giants in Folk Tales. Abraham Lincoln, himself a man of 6 foot 4 inches (1.93 meters!), uttered the following: " The eyes of that species of extinct giants whose bones fill the Mounds of America, have gazed on Niagara as ours do now." He knew that giants were roaming America! During the last centuries, there were numerous articles in newspapers about excavations of 3 – 4-meter skeletons all over America….You might have heard stories about Bigfoot? Sometimes he is a large, bloodthirsty monster that hunts men, women, and children. Some other times Bigfoot was known to protect humans with the ancient knowledge of natural medicine. These stories are known all over the US and the Flathead and Shoshone tribes share very similar stories. This is one of those stories:

"There were many giants but they were not as plentiful as us humans. We did not speak their language. There were giants that hated humans and would hunt them every chance they got, while others left humans alone and lived in solitude. They enjoyed a varied diet depending on where they lived, but they preferred the largest game like buffalo, deer, bear, large fish, etc. that could fill their bellies."

"There is a story of a man who went out hunting by himself, as he was walking on a ridge he slipped and fell down the ravine and was severely mangled. A giant found him and brought him back to his cave where he treated all his wounds. With his great knowledge of medicine, he cleaned and covered the wounds with a poultice and fed him medicine, within a few days the man was healed with no sight of a single scratch.

When he returned to his village he shared what he went through and who had helped him. After this time many people would leave gifts outside their lodges for the giant, thanking him for watching over him.

As a child my aunt brought me books of Fairy and Folk tales from all over the world, I was a voracious reader. Austria with its numerous mountains has a lot of old tales about giants, good or bad. Big people need big structures to hide from the world. One of the latest intriguing tales is the giant of Kandahar encountered by some US troops in Afghanistan. As there cannot be any proof unless you see a giant in front of you we must employ caution and reason – but a multitude of these tales might point to a grain of truth.

And all over the world there are gigantic, petrified stones and mountains to be found resembling people or animals – some of them are revered as sacred sites.

One famous one is the big snake Naka in Thailand, easily found on the net.
Another one of them is the sleeping lady of Mount Gulaga, a sacred aboriginal mountain
on the East coast of Australia, which resembles from a certain angle a body of a sleeping woman.
(Photo of The Sleeping Woman above)

Another petrified giant is visible beside Machu Picchu in Peru. My tour guide at the time even showed me a photo and told the story of a giant living there hundreds of years ago who lived peacefully with the people. The photo below shows a tranquil and even a smiling Giant. All facial features couldn't have been formed randomly by nature. What is your opinion, dear reader?

Above Sleeping Giant beside Machu Picchu in Peru

So there were good Giants and bad Giants but all in all the offspring of the fallen Angels were a rebellious group wanting to exert their own power and subjugate human beings. Their gods after the flood were Moloch and Baal and one of their favorite sacrifices was that of a child and even drinking the blood. These practices are detestable to the God of the Bible.

This is the reason that God sent the flood to wipe out evil.

Evidence today (Can easily be found on the net)

Geological evidence of fossilized Giants found all over earth. Fossilized big tree stumps can be seen all over America. Skeletons of Giants found and reported in newspapers A multitude of FB groups are sharing photos of old newspapers with reports of 3-metre-long skeletons being unearthed.

FB Groups sharing photos from the 18th century– very tall people still existed!

Below reproductions of Postcards and photos of the 18th century

God Exists - Evidence of Biblical Miracles Brought to Light

Noah's Ark

Everyone has heard of Noah's Ark. But have you ever heard that remnants of this Ark have been discovered in Turkey? This is the story of the Flood, the Ark, and its discovery.

Genesis 6:5 NIV

The Lord saw how great man's wickedness on the earth had become, and that every inclination of the thoughts of his heart was only evil all the time.

Genesis 6:12 NIV

God saw how corrupt the earth had become, for all the people on earth had corrupted their ways. So God said to Noah, "I am going to put an end to all people, for the earth is filled with violence because of them. I am surely going to destroy both them and the earth. So make yourself an ark of cypress wood, make rooms in it and coat it with pitch inside and out. This is how you are to build it: The ark is to be 450 feet long, 75 feet wide and 45 feet high."

It sounds ominous and we do not really know which kind of evil was dominating at that time. God hates the sacrifice of children, praying to other gods, sexual immorality, genetic engineering and splicing, creating other creatures, injustice for the poor. And God saw that every thought of the hearts of mankind was evil; it wasn't a good world to live in at that time.

The Book of Jasher or Jashar sheds some light on the kind of evil performed before the flood (also called The Book of Upright or the Book of Just Men). Some sources say that this book was once the original beginning of the Bible. It certainly contains a lot of stories about the old patriarchs. It was originally translated from Hebrew in A.D. 800, then suppressed and rediscovered in 1829 when it was once again suppressed.

This book is mentioned three times in the Old and New Testaments, so it is probably not a forgery. But make up your own mind and let the words sink in. I wonder why it was concealed; it is such an interesting book with lots of insights as you can see below.

Book of Jasher, Chapter 4:16-18

16 And all the sons of men departed from the ways of the Lord in those days as they multiplied upon the face of the earth with sons and daughters, and they taught one another their evil practices and they continued sinning against the Lord.

17 And every man made unto himself a god, and they robbed and plundered every man his neighbor as well as his relative, and they corrupted the earth, and the earth was filled with violence.

18 And their judges and rulers went to the daughters of men and took their wives by force from their husbands according to their choice, and the sons of men in those days took from the cattle of the earth, the beasts of the field and the fowls of the air, and taught the mixture of animals of one species with the other, in order therewith to provoke the Lord; and God saw the whole earth and it was corrupt, for all flesh had corrupted its ways upon earth, all men and all animals.

WHAT DID THEY DO? Every Man had an image of another god in his house, they were all dishonest with each other and even amongst relatives, their leaders and judges took wives away from other husbands as they pleased and to top it all off: they knew and performed genetic splicing and mixing different animals. If the leaders are corrupted, then it doesn't bode well for the rest of society. And don't mess with God's creation…

What would you have done to these people if you were the almighty God?

So God wanted to put an end to it but he rescued one good man and his family and this man was Noah. God gave Noah specific instructions on how to build the Ark and which materials to use. He also said to build a lower, middle and upper deck. And no, Noah wasn't a big giant. Divide 45 by three = 15 feet. 4,5 metres was the height for one level, so Noah could have been taller than a man of today. The grave of Noah's wife has been discovered and it seems that she was about that size. As we are today of a smaller size, I wondered if our conscience, heart, soul, mind, intelligence and everything we are might be less. Here is the answer:

2 Esdras 5 (Missing Books of the Bible)

51 He replied to me, "Ask a woman who bears children, and she will tell you.

52 Say to her, 'Why are those whom you have borne recently not like those whom you bore before, but smaller in stature?'

53 And she herself will answer you, 'Those born in the strength of youth are different from those born during the time of old age, when the womb is failing.'

54 Therefore you also should consider that you and your contemporaries are smaller in stature than those who were before you,

55 and those who come after you will be smaller than you, as born of a creation that already is aging and passing the strength of youth."

Interesting... it seems that we are of smaller size than our forefathers?

Only Noah and his wife, his three sons Shem, Ham and Japeth and their wives were allowed into the ark with every living animal, male and female.
Eight people survived the flood – all others perished. According to this testimony all of us are the descendents of Noah. Why fight each other, nation against nation, when we are all one family? If you wonder how elephants, lions, snakes, gazelles and all kinds of animals would have remained in a tranquil state for 150 days in an ark – there might have been only little cubs of the dangerous animals and all was organised like a well kept Zoo. Maybe Noah had some herbs or smoke which put dangerous species into sleep for the time being? Imagine you would have been selected – such an honor – and then you were living in an enclosed house on water and in bad weather – no stepping out and smelling the fresh air – the responsiblity of feeding all the livestock and being of good cheer after all your family, friends, people were drowned in the flood waters. We watch disaster movies all the time and find them exhilarating but it is a different story when you experience the perishing of all you knew, or?

Genesis 8:4 NIV... *and on the seventeenth day of the seventh month the Ark came to rest on the mountains of Ararat...*

This was quite a long time ago and the question is: Did it really happen? All over our earth tribes have old tales about a big deluge.
In Aztec mythology, Coxcox and his wife, Xochiquetzel, survived the flood. They took refuge in the hollow trunk of a cypress, which floated on top of the water and finally banked on a mountain in Culhuacan.
Of course all the names are different to the ones in the Bible. After the flood when the tower of Babel was build as the people wanted to reach Heaven and destroy God, God simply confused them by letting the people forget their original language and from one day to the next people were speaking different tongues and couldn't understand each other.
So – what of the Ark – has it been found? Several supposed arks have been located but it seems that only Ron Wyatt was truly guided by God and he established with supporting evidence that it was Noah's Ark which slid down the mountains of Ararat– and his findings were true to the measurements written in the Bible.
May I introduce Ron Wyatt to you – a faithful man from Tenessee who worked tirelessly and with his own money to discover the Ark and the Chariots in the Red Sea and more. Ron read the Bible and also believed that it was not only scripture to be interpreted in an allegorical context. He prayed to God for a way he could be of service and a few days later he saw a a photo of the Ark published in Life Magazine in 1959, in which topographical photos shot by a surveyor during the Cold War showed the imprints of a vessel near the mountains of Ararat. Ron did explore and research further but it took him 16 years to visit the mountains of Ararat in Turkey for the first time.

This was in 1977 and he and his sons didn't know where to begin searching when with a driver, exploring the vast mountain ranges. They only had three days! The picture in Life Magazine had no reference for the location.

This is a recount of their discovery:
After the first day of driving through the mountainous terrain, they found nothing. While they were driving back to the hotel after nightfall Ron said, "We should all say a prayer which way to look tomorrow." So they prayed. A few minutes later the car shut down and despite checking under the hood no fault was found. Then the car just started again. Out of curiosity, Ron marked the spot with a rock pile. This happened twice again on their way back– and Ron marked each car stop with a pile of rocks. When they drove back on the next day they found all three piles – each pile pointing to something special. They found a big Anchor Stone with eight Crosses inscribed. The next pile was near a house and a graveyard. On the tombstone was a drawing of eight people and a boat below. The third pile was on the site of Noah's Ark. It was amazing for all three to have their prayers answered instantly and with each pile of rock showcasing the evidence of the Ark.

Over the next years, Ron obtained permission from the Turkish Government to excavate and he and his team found evidence of structure, metal support, and even some animal remains inside the Ark. Around that area are thirty big Drogue Stones scattered around. These stones were used to leverage boats in ancient times and these are the biggest found on earth which supports the evidence for the biggest ship ever built; they are also not near any port but instead landlocked with 200 km distance east and west to the coast. Underground scanning of the site revealed a big structure that looked like a big shipwreck with a deep hull design.

In 2019 radar scans revealed the presence of straight lines and a manmade ship-like structure. The internal features match exactly the dimensions mentioned in the Bible using the Egyptian cubit as a unit of measure. Mount Ararat is in Eastern Turkey and Turkey does now acknowledge the location of the Ark; it is signposted as a National Park with a Tourist building and nearby is an ancient stone, some say from the Sumerian time, which has simple carvings of four men and four women in a big boat.

According to my old Holy Bible (by James McKay, Sydney, 1873) Genesis or the Creation happened 4004 years before Christ was born. The Flood happened in the year 2349 BC. After the flood these eight survivors multiplied again and evil thoughts and aspirations took a foothold again. But God gave us a covenant that a deluge of this magnitude would never happen again:

Genesis 8:22 (NIV)

"As long as the earth endures, seedtime and harvest, cold and heat, summer and winter, day and night will never cease."

And Genesis 9:13 -15 (NIV)

"I have set my rainbow in the clouds, and it will be the sign of the covenant between me and the earth. Whenever I bring clouds over the earth and the rainbow appears in the clouds, I will remember my covenant between me and you and all living creatures of every kind. Never again will the waters become a flood to destroy all life."

Evidence today

The site of the Ark has been measured and scanned and undeniably resembles a ship. A probe inside the Ark found animal hair, animal dropping and a petrified deer's antler. A laminated piece of wood with tiny nails has been unearthed and thoroughly tested. Thirty Drogue stones are scattered around the area; holes where the ship's rope would have been attached are still visible in some of them today.

Sodom and Gomorrah

Do you know the story of Sodom and Gomorrah, two cities after the flood where life has been wiped out because of the evil practiced in these cities? The Lord himself came down to earth and visited Abraham. At the end of their meeting the Lord said, *"The outcry against Sodom and Gomorrah is so great and their sin so grievous that I will go down and see if what they have done is as bad as the outcry that has reached me. If not, I will know."* (Genesis 18:20 NIV)

So God came down personally to visit these two cities to see if the people living there were wicked. And Abraham started to plead with God and asked if the cities could be spared if only fifty or forty-five or forty or even only ten righteous people could be found. But there were not even ten righteous people to be found… This happened after the flood – people multiplied and did evil again in God's sight.

When reading about Sodom and Gomorrah in the past I had this unquenchable curiosity and thirst for knowledge about the real evil the inhabitants of these cities performed. What was so detestable to the Lord that he had to destroy all living souls except one man and his wife and his two daughters? The entire Bible of today does not explain in detail what this evil was.

But the Book of Jasher does!

The Book of Jasher contains the most detailed descriptions of the patriarchs' lives after the flood and it is unlikely in my opinion that all is purely invented. There is a very good Audio version read by Christopher Glyn available on YouTube.

Book of Jasher, Chapter 19

1 And the cities of Sodom had four judges to four cities, and these were their names, Serak in the city of Sodom, Sharkad in Gomorrah, Zabnac in Admah, and Menon in Zeboyim.

3 And by desire of their four judges the people of Sodom and Gomorrah had beds erected in the streets of the cities, and if a man came to these places they laid hold of him and brought him to one of their beds, and by force made him to lie in them.

4 And as he lay down, three men would stand at his head and three at his feet, and measure him by the length of the bed, and if the man was less than the bed these six men would stretch him at each end, and when he cried out to them they would not answer him.

5 And if he was longer than the bed they would draw together the two sides of the bed at each end, until the man had reached the gates of death.

6 And if he continued to cry out to them, they would answer him, saying, Thus shall it be done to a man that cometh into our land.

7 And when men heard all these things that the people of the cities of Sodom did, they refrained from coming there.

8 And when a poor man came to their land they would give him silver and gold, and cause a proclamation in the whole city not to give him a morsel of bread to eat, and if the stranger should remain there some days, and die from hunger, not having been able to obtain a morsel of bread, then at his death all the people of the city would come and take their silver and gold which they had given to him.

9 And those that could recognize the silver or gold which they had given him took it back, and at his death they also stripped him of his garments, and they would fight about them, and he that prevailed over his neighbor took them.

10 They would after that carry him and bury him under some of the shrubs in the deserts; so they did all the days to anyone that came to them and died in their land.

24 At that time the wife of Lot bares him a daughter, and he called her name Paltith, saying, Because God had delivered him and his whole household from the kings of Elam; and Paltith daughter of Lot grew up, and one of the men of Sodom took her for a wife.

25 And a poor man came into the city to seek a maintenance, and he remained in the city some days, and all the people of Sodom caused a proclamation of their custom not to give this man a morsel of bread to eat, until he dropped dead upon the earth, and they did so.

26 And Paltith the daughter of Lot saw this man lying in the streets starved with hunger, and no one would give him anything to keep him alive, and he was just upon the point of death.

27 And her soul was filled with pity on account of the man, and she fed him secretly with bread for many days, and the soul of this man was revived.

28 For when she went forth to fetch water she would put the bread in the water pitcher, and when she came to the place where the poor man was, she took the bread from the pitcher and gave it him to eat; so she did many days.

29 And all the people of Sodom and Gomorrah wondered how this man could bear starvation for so many days.

30 And they said to each other, This can only be that he eats and drinks, for no man can bear starvation for so many days or live as this man has, without even his countenance changing; and three men concealed themselves in a place where the poor man was stationed, to know who it was that brought him bread to eat.

31 And Paltith daughter of Lot went forth that day to fetch water, and she put bread into her pitcher of water, and she went to draw water by the poor man's place, and she took out the bread from the pitcher and gave it to the poor man and he ate it.

32 And the three men saw what Paltith did to the poor man, and they said to her, It is thou then who hast supported him, and therefore has he not starved, nor changed in appearance nor died like the rest.

33 And the three men went out of the place in which they were concealed, and they seized Paltith and the bread which was in the poor man's hand.

34 And they took Paltith and brought her before their judges, and they said to them, Thus did she do, and it is she who supplied the poor man with bread, therefore did he not die all this time; now therefore declare to us the punishment due to this woman for having transgressed our law.

35 And the people of Sodom and Gomorrah assembled and kindled a fire in the street of the city, and they took the woman and cast her into the fire and she was burned to ashes.

36 And in the city of Admah there was a woman to whom they did the like.

37 For a traveler came into the city of Admah to abide there all night, with the intention of going home in the morning, and he sat opposite the door of the house of the young woman's father, to remain there, as the sun had set when he had reached that place; and the young woman saw him sitting by the door of the house.

38 And he asked her for a drink of water and she said to him, Who art thou? and he said to her, I was this day going on the road, and reached here when the sun set, so I will abide here all night, and in the morning I will arise early and continue my journey.

39 And the young woman went into the house and fetched the man bread and water to eat and drink.

40 And this affair became known to the people of Admah, and they assembled and brought the young

woman before the judges, that they should judge her for this act.

41 And the judge said, The judgment of death must pass upon this woman because she transgressed our law, and this therefore is the decision concerning her.

42 And the people of those cities assembled and brought out the young woman, and anointed her with honey from head to foot, as the judge had decreed, and they placed her before a swarm of bees which were then in their hives, and the bees flew upon her and stung her that her whole body was swelled.

43 And the young woman cried out on account of the bees, but no one took notice of her or pitied her, and her cries ascended to heaven.

44 And the Lord was provoked at this and at all the works of the cities of Sodom, for they had abundance of food, and had tranquility amongst them, and still would not sustain the poor and the needy, and in those days their evil doings and sins became great before the Lord.

45 And the Lord sent for two of the angels that had come to Abraham's house, to destroy Sodom and its cities.

Crazy!

This is a lot to digest.

So- A visitor to these cities would be stripped of his possessions and stretched or crushed to death openly in the street for everyone to see. Or the visitor would receive gold or silver but nothing to eat or drink and the citizens would watch until this visitor had died and then take the gold and strip the man of all clothing.

And the two women who secretly gave two men some water and bread were declared guilty by the judges of these cities and then received a death sentence. This was pure evil and not a code of conduct God would like to see perpetuated for future generations. So he wiped them out. Interesting to observe that the woman stung by bees cried out to Heaven and God heard her – and acted upon it. Prayer can do that.

So Sodom and Gomorrah were destroyed and an Angel rescued only Abraham's nephew Lot, his wife and their two daughters. Unfortunately Lot's wife was disobedient to the Angel's instructions and looked around when the destruction happened – she turned into a pillar of stone. Search 'Lot's wife pillar of stone' and you can find photos on the net.

Sodom and Gomorrah and the three other cities were found in 1989 by Ron Wyatt and the evidence is staggering. Here on earth it is the only location where sulfur balls in their purest form are found. These balls have a content of 96 - 98% pure sulfur and this should be proof enough that God's punishment for wicked people really happened.

The cities were located in the plain on the border of the Dead Sea and today there are still remnants of ziggurats, sphinxes and other formations, which without doubt were buildings before the destruction. It's actually quite vast and desolate, big structures stripped with just a skeleton remaining, clearly visible in a few YouTube videos circulating, for example by Timo Shely and KJV pictures.

These cities were still well known in the first century as the historian Josephus remarked: "The traces or shadows of the five cities are still to be seen." And almost 2000 years later the scenery as described by Josephus is unchanged!

Genesis 19:24 -25 NIV:

Then the Lord rained down burning sulfur on Sodom and Gomorrah – from the Lord out of the heavens. Thus he overthrew those cities and the entire plain, including all those living in the cities- and also the vegetation in the land.

And up until now there has been a desolate landscape with nothing much growing. God can make land fertile or desolate.

Simon Peter, one of the apostles of Jesus Christ, wrote an interesting conclusion about this extermination in

2 Peter 2:6 – 9 NIV

… if he condemned the cities of Sodom and Gomorrah by burning them to ashes, and made them an example of what is going to happen to the ungodly; and if he rescued Lot, a righteous man, who was distressed by the filthy lives of lawless men (for that righteous man, living among them day after day, was tormented in his righteous soul by the lawless deeds he saw and heard) – if this is so, then the Lord knows how to rescue godly men from trials and hold the unrighteous for the day of the judgement, while continuing their punishment.

All over this world lawlessness in the name of democracy or otherwise is flourishing. Please search in your heart for God, hold on to his word and he will sustain you through difficult times, even war. This I believe.

The way to Hell is easy.

You can do anything you want in life – hurting someone, cheating, lying and giving a false testimony – and maybe you are not caught. But then you go to Hell for eternity. That might not be easy and it is forever. The way to Heaven is more difficult.

You must be good and love your neighbor, don't hate even your enemies, obey the commands and precepts of God and Jesus, forgive everything which has been wrongfully done to you and ask for forgiveness for the things you have done wrong.

You must believe in God and Jesus. Then you go to Heaven and I imagine Heaven a joyful place.

The painting above depicts artistically the flow of swirls caused through the burning sulfur balls, etching these patterns into the remnants of citadels and houses. You can look up the real image on the web on Ron Wyatt's own website.

This happened 1898 BC. (Holy Bible, printed by James McKay, Sydney, 1873)

Evidence today

Geological evidence of burnt and unburnt sulfur balls all over the four cities. Big structures, ziggurats and sphinxes are still standing today. Structures and walls have swirled ash formations etched on the buildings. Desolate landscape.

The Exodus – and The Chariots in the Red Sea

This is the story of God's people brought to Egypt because of a big food shortage – and after his people endured the hardship of slavery God brought his flock back to the promised land, performing miracle after miracle.

Joseph brought the Israelites out of their land into Egypt because of a big famine.

He was one of Jacob's twelve sons. His father loved him more than any of the others and gave him a coloured cloak. Therefore his brothers were jealous of him and sold him into slavery. He then was taken to Egypt, spent time in prison for a crime he did not commit and eventually became steward to Potiphar, one of Pharaoh's officials.

Joseph helped the Pharaoh of Egypt to collect grain in seven good years as God told him what was about to happen and Pharaoh listened to Joseph. Seven bountiful years passed followed by seven years of famine and Pharaoh was grateful to Joseph and let him bring his eleven brothers and all their wives and family to reside in Egypt. 430 years later the situation for the Israelites looked very different; they were enslaved by the Egyptians and had to do hard labor – and their number had increased to over one million people. Moses asked the Pharaoh to release the Israelites to pray for a few days in the desert but Pharaoh refused. Then God sent ten different plagues to Egypt and finally Pharaoh relented and let the Israelites go with parting gifts of gold and fine cloth from the Egyptians.

Afterwards, Pharaoh changed his mind and pursued the Israelites with his army and chariots. The Israelites were enslaved until then and not trained in warfare nor did they have weapons and they were afraid. They came to the Red Sea and couldn't cross it without boats.

But God had a solution as always:

Exodus 14:15 – 31 NIV

Then the Lord said to Moses, "Why are you crying out to me? Tell the Israelites to move on. Raise your staff and stretch out your hand over the sea to divide the water so that the Israelites can go through the sea on dry ground. I will harden the hearts of the Egyptians so that they will go in after them. And I will gain glory through Pharaoh and all his army, through his chariots and his horsemen. The Egyptians will know that I am the Lord when I gain glory through Pharaoh, his chariots and his horsemen.

Then the angel of God, who had been travelling in front of Israel's army, withdrew and went behind them. The pillar of cloud also moved from in front and stood behind them, coming between the armies of Egypt and Israel. Throughout the night the cloud brought darkness to one side and light to the other side: so neither went near the other all night long.

Then Moses stretched out his hand over the sea, and all that night the Lord drove the sea back with a strong east wind and turned it into dry land. The waters were divided, and the Israelites went through the sea on dry ground, with a wall of water on their right and on their left.

The Egyptians pursued them, and all Pharaoh's horses and chariots and horsemen followed them into the sea. During the last watch of the night the Lord looked down from the pillar of fire and cloud at the Egyptian army and threw them into confusion. He made the wheels of the chariots come off so they had difficulty driving. And the Egyptians said," Let's get away from the Israelites! The Lord is fighting for them against Egypt.' Then the Lord said to Moses," Stretch out your hand over the sea so that the waters may flow back over the Egyptians and their chariots and horsemen.' Moses stretched out his hand over the sea, and at daybreak the sea went back to its place. The Egyptians were fleeing toward it, and the Lord swept them into the sea. The water flowed back and covered the chariots and the horsemen – the entire army of Pharaoh that had followed the Israelites into the sea. Not one of them survived. But the Israelites went through the sea on dry ground, with a humongous wall of water on each side. That day the Lord saved Israel from the hand of the Egyptians, and Pharaoh's army was lying like dead fish on the shore. And when the Israelites realized the power the Lord displayed against the Egyptians, the people feared the Lord and put their trust in him and in Moses his servant.

If you, your family and your dog or cat had been part of this tribe and had hastened securely through this tunnel on the seabed – then this would have been etched in your mind as some experience you surely would never forget and credit the Lord for?

As a boon the dead bodies of Pharaoh washed up with their weapons strapped to their backs and the Israelites only had to collect these and suddenly they possessed valuable armor for fighting the enemies they would encounter later.

There is no biblical reference of this. However, Jewish historian Josephus found the following in Book II, chapter 16 of the *Antiquities of the Jews:* 'After Pharaoh's army was destroyed in the Red Sea, Moses ordered the Israelites to pick up the armor and weapons from the dead Egyptians whose bodies washed up on the shore. On the next day (after the parting of the Red Sea) Moses gathered together the weapons of the Egyptians, which were brought to the camp of the Hebrews by the current of the sea, and the force of the winds resisting it; and he conjectured that this also happened by divine providence, that so they might not be destitute of weapons. So when he had ordered the Hebrews to arm themselves with them, he led them to Mount Sinai, in order to offer sacrifice to God, and to render oblations for the salvation of the multitude, as he was charged to do beforehand.'

Numerous attempts to find the crossing site were fruitless but Ron Wyatt had been guided and found the site at the Gulf of Aqaba in 1978, when he and his sons, Danny and Ronny, made two trips to Israel in order to drive down to the western shore of the Gulf of Aqaba in Egypt. This was during the time that Israel was occupying the Sinai Peninsula.

He did dive into the waters and found remnants of chariots and wheels, some overgrown with corals and even one golden wheel, the gold on the wooden structure still intact. The underwater footage is riveting! There are no other coral reefs apart from the corals on the remnants of the 2,000 chariots, wheels upright in unnatural positions and even remnants of human bones. Vivek Ponten also dived and searched on the forbidden Saudi Arab side and found chariot remnants overgrown with coral.

This crossing site is the shallowest part in the whole Gulf of Aqaba. The downhill slope on one site and the uphill slope on the other side were manageable by horse and cart!

The Exodus happened in the year 1491 BC according to my old Holy Bible. You can see the photos of the discoveries on Ron Wyatt's website and all over the Internet – this is truly a miracle still visible over 3,500 years later preserved under the sea of the Gulf of Aqaba. On one side of the shore is a stele in memory of this crossing erected by King Solomon still standing today.

'The Exodus', Diptych, Oil on Canvas, each canvas 160 x 160 cm

Evidence today

Underwater remnants of chariot wheels overgrown with coral. The area in front of the crossing was and is big enough to serve as a campsite for one million people. Shallow passage where crossing was possible with not too steep inclines. A column erected on one side – Solomon's column to commemorate the crossing still standing today.

And Paul wrote in Galatians 4:25:

*Now Hagar stands for **Mount Sinai in Arabia** and corresponds….*

The Split Rock of Rephidim

The Israelites wandered in the desert for forty years before God led them into the Promised Land.

Exodus 17:1-7 NIV

The whole Israelite community set out from the Desert of Sin, traveling from place to place as the Lord commanded. They camped at Rephidim, but there was no water for the people to drink. So they quarreled with Moses and said, "Give us water to drink." Moses replied, " Why do you quarrel with me? Why do you put the Lord to the test?" But the people were thirsty for water and they grumbled against Moses. They said, "Why did you bring us out of Egypt to make us and our children and livestock die of thirst?"
Then Moses cried out to the Lord, "What am I to do with these people? They are almost ready to stone me."
The Lord answered Moses, "Walk on ahead of the people? Take with you some of the people of Israel and take in your hand the staff with which you struck the Nile, and go. I will stand there before you by the rock at Horeb. Strike the rock and water will come out of it for the people to drink."
So Moses did this in the sight of the elders of Israel. And he called the place Massah and Meribab because the Israelites quarreled and because they tested the Lord saying,
"Is the Lord among us or not?"

There are more passages in the Bible referring to this miracle:

Psalms 78.15-16

He split the rocks in the desert. And gave them water as abundant as the seas; he brought streams out of a rocky crag and made water flow down like rivers.

Isaiah 48.21

They did not thirst when he led them through the deserts; he made water flow for them from the rock; he split the rock and water gushed out.

These were the same people who were a few days before rescued by many miracles and led through a dry passage in the midst of the Red Sea into safety.
Would you have grumbled or prayed to the Lord for water? He just performed a big miracle for you and annihilated a powerful army, only to let you die of thirst? A bit of trust was required here, just like for us believers today.
Estimates of Bible historians record that there were over 1 million people and their livestock moving through the desert. They were fed with quail (another one of these miracles without evidence today) and now needed water – a huge amount of water – and God provided water from a big rock.

Where is this massive rock located? Is it still there today? There is some historical documentation that the Split Rock of Horeb was known and identifiable in the 1700s AD.
William Whitson, who translated Josephus' works, wrote a footnote as follows: 'This rock is there at this day, as the travelers agree; and must be the same that was there in the days of Moses, as being too large to be brought thither by our modern carriages.' Quite a funny remark actually!
There is a massive, visually stunning split rock located northwest of Jabal Maqla along a possible route to the mountain. It stands approximately 50 feet tall on top of a hill that is approximately 100 feet high. The split in the middle is sizable enough for a person to stand inside it.
This giant split rock was re-discovered in the 1990s by Jimmy and Penny Caldwell who were stationed with their children for twelve years in Saudi Arabia and secretly did numerous trips to this site, finding not only the mountain of God, Mount Horeb, but also other evidence which supports that this was once the site where over a million Israelites camped on their way to the promised land.
The inside of the split rock is smooth and there appear to be washed-out paths downwards from the

split. The ground level on both sides of the hill is smooth and uneven, giving the visual appearance of former water rivulets having been there. It appears distinct from the rougher terrain that surrounds the site. Local Saudi Bedouins told the Caldwell's that it was known as "Moses' Water". Others who have visited the area have been more explicitly told that it is the "Split Rock of Moses". When asked about the source of that name, the Bedouins said it's been called that for generations.

Ron Wyatt also located the rock at Rephidim and came to the same conclusions as the Caldwells. Whilst he was searching in Saudi Arabia he was imprisoned for 21 days and accused of being an Israeli spy.

The hill at Rephidim rises 34 meters (110 feet) and on its top towers the huge upright rock, jutting another 15 meters (50 feet) into the air, in all a height equivalent to a 16-storey building. Still today the split rock can be seen standing high above the flat floor of the desert, a great testimony to the mighty works of God.

The whole Bible is filled with symbolism, and God is symbolized by a Rock.

"He is the Rock, his work is perfect, and all his ways are justified . A faithful God who does no wrong, upright and just is he."
(Deuteronomy 32:4 NIV)

"For their rock is not as our Rock, as even our enemies concede."(Deuteronomy 32:31 NIV)

"And he said, The Lord is my rock, my fortress and my deliverer; my God is my rock, in whom I take refuge, my shield and my horn of my salvation. He is my stronghold, my refuge and my savior-
(2 Samuel 22:2 NIV)

"The Lord is my rock, my fortress and my deliverer; my God is my rock, in whom I take refuge.
He is my shield and the horn of my salvation, my stronghold."
Psalms 18:2.

Evidence today

The Split Rock of Rephidim is still standing today, clearly visible, in Saudi Arabia.
The rock is smooth inside and had water flowing out.
Base of Golden Calf Altar still standing, fenced by the Saudi Arabian Government.
Etchings in rocks are visible today with calves and also menorahs
(menorahs mostly scratched out but visible on older videos).
A corral for livestock is still visible today.
Big stones with mortar indentures on which the Israelites were grinding their
morning manna strewn around.
Markers around Mount Horeb

Mount Horeb

This is the mountain where God gave Moses the Ten Commandments. It is a special mountain with a crust of black at the top because God descended on this mountain for quite a while and the top of the mountain was burnt.

Exodus 19:1-2 NIV

In the third month after the Israelites left Egypt - on the very day- they came to the desert of Sinai. After they set out from Rephidim, they entered the desert of Sinai, and Israel camped there in the desert in front of the mountain.

Moses went up this mountain and met God, who instructed him to keep his covenant and promised in return that the Israelites would be treasured as his holy people. So Moses went back and conveyed the message to the people and they all responded together that they would do everything the Lord has said. Then God demanded of Moses that he consecrate the people and that they wash their clothes.

Exodus 19:16 – 22 NIV

On the morning of the third day there was thunder and lightning. Then Moses led the people out of the camp to meet with God, and they stood at the foot of the mountain, with a thick cloud over the mountain, and a very loud trumpet blast. Everyone in the camp trembled.
Mount Sinai was covered with smoke, because the Lord descended on it in fire. The smoke billowed up from it like smoke from a furnace, the whole mountain trembled violently, and the sound of the trumpet grew louder and louder. Then Moses spoke and the voice of God answered him.

Moses went up the mountain and meanwhile the one million Israelites who fled through the Red Sea to escape the pursuit of Pharaoh were dissatisfied with being left alone and demanded of Aaron, the brother of Moses and chief-priest, to build an idol.

Aaron was too afraid to refuse this request and demanded all gold to be collected – and then they built a Golden Calf, an idol and abomination to God, all in plain sight of his holy mountain. They danced around this idol and this is detestable to the Lord.

When Moses finally came down the mountain carrying the Ten Commandments written by God he was so angry because he saw the people dancing and revelling (which means probably being drunk and also having intercourse) that he lost his temper and smashed the two tablets...

God also was wrathful with this and demanded that people who believed in him to congregate at one site – these were the Levites who then strapped swords to their side and killed 3,000 Israelites on that day. It is a sad event when brother kills brother.

Later Moses went up the mountain again and God was merciful and wrote two new tablets with the same commandments.

The TEN Commandments

- **I am your God. You shall not have other gods beside me.**
- **You shall not worship any idol or make any idols.**
- **You shall not take my name in vain.**
- **You shall honour the Sabbath and not work.**
- **You shall honour your father and mother.**
- **You shall not kill.**
- **You shall not commit adultery.**
- **You shall not steal.**
- **You shall not bear false witness.**
- **You shall not covet your neighbour's wife or possessions.**

These are the Ten Commandments given to Moses for us to live by still today and this is the mountain where God descended personally amidst a big fire and trembling and the sound of trumpets.

Where is this mountain today?

Saudi Arabia has posed strict restrictions and is threatening visitors with jail. Despite this, different parties have dared to enter Saudi Arabia and believe they have discovered God's mountain.

Robert Cornuke and Larry Williams went there in 1988. Both found afterwards a wealth of information from university libraries, which also overwhelmingly leaned in favor of Jabal al Lawz (Mount Horeb) as being the real Mount Sinai.

Dr. Allan Kerkeslager wrote to Larry Williams: " You will be pleased to find that you have some good, solid evidence for your views. A Jewish tradition dating to at least 250 BC… identified Mount Sinai with the highest mountain near ancient Madyan, which is the modern town of Al-bad. The most likely candidate, I have concluded, is Jabal al-Lawz."

Evidence today

Mount Horeb has its peak covered with black. This is not volcanic activity but consists of a black crust formed around all hard materials.
The markers were found around Mount Horeb to deter the Israelites from coming too close.
The altar of the golden calf is still visible and massive in size.

The Budding of Aaron's Staff

At one time during their journey through the desert there was dissent and insolence against Aaron and Moses again. A few rebellious men and their followers contested the leadership of these two men. Moses was very angry with this and relayed the matter to God who wanted to put an end to these wicked men, all 250 of them.

Moses and Aaron intervened and God relented and only the dissident leaders and their families were punished. God just opened the earth and these sinners and their tents were swallowed and disappeared. Sorry, there is no archaeological evidence of this to be found except some gravestones scattered around. If we believe that some of these miracles have happened, then we can also believe all of them happened.

This is the passage of the ensuing miracle where God did elect the priestly leader of the Israelites.

Numbers 17:1 - 11 NIV

The Lord said to Moses, "Speak to the Israelites and get twelve staffs from them, one from the leader of each of their ancestral tribes. Write the name of each man on his staff. On the staff of Levi write Aaron's name, for there must be one staff for the head of each ancestral tribe. Place them in the tent of Meeting in front of the Testimony, where I meet with you. The staff belonging to the man I choose will sprout, and I will rid myself of this constant grumbling against you by the Israelites."

So Moses spoke to the Israelites, and their leaders gave him twelve staffs, one for the leader of each of their ancestral tribes, and Aaron's staff was among them. Moses placed their staffs before the Lord in the Tent of the Testimony.

The next day Moses entered the Tent of the Testimony and saw that Aaron's staff, which represented the house of Levi, had not only sprouted but had budded, blossomed and produced almonds. Then Moses brought out all the staffs from the Lord's presence to all the Israelites. They looked at them and each man took his own staff.

The Lord said to Moses,

"Put back Aaron's staff in front of the Testimony, to be kept as a sign to the rebellious. This will put an end to the grumbling against me, so that they will not die."

Moses did just as the Lord commanded him.

God knew exactly which staff to select and the next day the chosen one was budding with almond blossoms, also fruiting with almonds and it must have been a beautiful sight! It was Aaron's staff.

Neither you nor I could have done this within a day. Of course there is no evidence of this miracle. But why wouldn't it have been true?

And all-around Mount Horeb there are almond bushes still blossoming and budding today according to Jim and Penny Caldwell.

Evidence today

None – Except the occurrence of Almond bushes in this area still today

The Prophet Elijah

Imagine loving and serving God so much that God selects you to be a prophet in a time when neither kings nor people worship or follow God very much. The prophet Elijah was living in that time and he had to deliver very unpleasant messages from God to a bad king. The king allowed the existence of worship to the Baals, other gods made out of stone and without power.

Elijah's message from God was to invite all the prophets of the Baals to have a contest.

1 KINGS 18:20 – 24

So Ahab sent word throughout all Israel and assembled the prophets on Mount Carmel. Elijah went before the people and said, "How long will you waver between two opinions? If the Lord is God, follow him; but if Baal is God, follow him." But the people said nothing.

Then Elijah said to them, "I am the only one of the Lord's prophets left, but Baal has four hundred and fifty prophets. Get two bulls for us. Let them choose one for themselves, and let them cut it into pieces and put it on the wood but not set fire to it. Then you call on the name of your god, and I will call on the name of the Lord. The god who answers by fire – he is God."
Then all the people said, "What you say is good."

The four hundred fifty prophets called on the name of Baal from morning till noon. Midday passed, and they continued their frantic prophesying until the time for the evening sacrifice. But there was no response, no one answered, no one paid attention.
Elijah then repaired the altar of the Lord, which was in ruins. He arranged the wood, cut the bull into pieces and laid it on the wood. He even said,

"Fill four large jars with water and pour it on the offering and on the wood."

1 KINGS 18:36 – 40

At the time of the sacrifice, the prophet Elijah stepped forward and prayed: "Oh Lord, God of Abraham, Isaac and Israel, let it be known that you are God in Israel and that I am your servant and have done all these things at your command. Answer me, O Lord, answer me, so these people will know that you, O Lord, are God, and that you are turning their hearts back again."
Then the fire of the Lord fell and burned up the sacrifice, the wood, the stones and the soil, and also licked up the water in the trench.
When all the people saw this, they fell prostrate and cried, "The Lord – he is God! The Lord – he is God!"
Then Elijah commanded them, "Seize the prophets of Baal. Don't let anyone get away!" They seized them, and Elijah had them brought down to the Kishon Valley and slaughtered there.

Jezebel, the very evil mother of the king at that time, threatened Elijah then and Elijah was anxious and ran for his life.

1 KINGS 19:2

So Jezebel sent a messenger to Elijah to say, "May the gods deal with me, be it ever so severely, if by this time tomorrow I do not make sure your life like that one of them." How would you have felt if you had ordered the killing of four hundred fifty evil prophets? Jezebel believed in other multiple gods and was evil; Elijah did all in the name of God and with a pure heart. Nevertheless, he was afraid and went into the desert. There he sat down under a broom tree and prayed that he might die. When he fell asleep an angel touched him and said, *"Get up and eat."*

1 KINGS 19:6

He looked around, and there by his head was a cake of bread baked over hot coals, and a jar of water. He ate and drank and then lay down again. The angel of the Lord came back a second time and touched him and said, "Get up and eat, for the journey is too much for you." So he got up and ate and drank. Strengthened by that food, he travelled forty days and forty nights until he reached Horeb, the mountain of God. There he went into a cave and spent the night.

All alone, Elijah then had an encounter with God.

Read it for yourselves if you want.

1 KINGS 20:15

The Lord said to him. "Go back the way you came, and go to the desert of Damascus. When you get there, anoint Hazael king over Aram. Also, anoint Jehu son of Nimshi king over Israel, and anoint Elisha son of Shaphat from Abel Meholah to succeed you as a prophet. Jehu will put to death any who escape the sword of Hazael, and Elisha will put to death any who escape the sword of Jehu. Yet I reserve seven thousand in Israel – all whose knee have not bowed down to Baal and all whose mouths have not kissed him."

So God took extra care that his people who believed in him stayed safe. He safeguarded those who did not bow down to any other god and did not follow any orders about worship. They remained steadfast in their belief and conduct to God and would not bow to any false idols and gods.

Today is not different to that time and God is omnipotent in caring and sheltering and protecting his children of a pure heart and conduct. Elijah was a prophet and a man and in a world full of evil he was afraid and then comforted by our Lord. An angel gave him food and this sounds miraculous.

Still, Elijah did not have a comfortable bed to sleep in; the cave had no TV or other amenities. He was alone and only comforted by his faith and God.

This cave depicted on the next page was painted from an image which Penny and Jim Caldwell took when exploring Mount Horeb – Yes, there is a cave at Mount Horeb and has been discovered by the Caldwells and it might have been the place were Elijah slept and all this happened 906 years before Christ was born according to my old Bible.

Evidence today

The Mountain commonly accepted as the Mount Sinai in Egypt doesn't have a cave.
Mount Horeb (the real Mount Sinai) features one cave, which could have been Elijah's cave.

No other evidence.

The Ark of the Covenant

What is the Ark of the Covenant?

The movie 'Raiders of the lost Ark' tells the story of Indiana Jones hired by the US Government to find the Ark of the Covenant before the Nazis can obtain the Ark and its powers.

I don't think God would have given his precious object into the hands of either party, because the Ark is the holiest of holies ever created by God here on earth. He designed this vessel himself and stipulated its materials. The Ark is inlaid and covered entirely with gold. Two cherubim are standing on each side, protecting the Ark with their wings. Inside are three items:

- A jar with manna which was the bread falling from heaven for forty years. feeding the Israelites during their Exodus

- The Ten Commandments written on two stone tablets Moses received on Mount Horeb

- Aaron's staff.

No one was allowed to touch the Ark of the Covenant, the Ark was moved from place to place with poles. On more than one occasion those who violated this law were struck dead. It also followed the Israelites into war and when the Ark was captured the enemy was struck down by a plague until they returned the Ark to the Israelites. (1 Samuel 5:9 NIV) God would have taken much care to secrete the Ark away until it would surface at the appointed time.

There have been searches for this holy Ark and there are several mainstream publications circulating about the current location of the Ark. The question is, where is the most likely spot on earth where God would have hidden his Ark?

This is a recount of Ron Wyatt's discovery:

In 1978 when Ron was on his second dive trip to search for the chariots in the Red Sea he was harmed by the sun's rays in the water whilst swimming for hours at a depth about 30 feet and searching the sea floor for more evidence. His legs and feet became painfully swollen to such an extent that he couldn't even get his fins on.

Unable to dive anymore, and with no motel in the area, he and his sons had no choice but to return to Jerusalem to wait until their flight from Tel Aviv left for the US. A few days after the swelling in Ron's leg had subsided he decided to go sightseeing around his hotel near the Damascus gate. Walking along the ancient stone quarry, known to some as 'The Calvary Escarpment', he started a conversation with someone who actually was a local authority on Roman antiquities. And then something extraordinary happened: Ron's left hand pointed to a site being used as a trash dump and he stated,

"That's Jeremiah's Grotto and the Ark of the Covenant is in there."

Even though these words had come from his own mouth and his hand had pointed, he had not consciously uttered these words. This was the first time that the Ark of the Covenant came to his mind.

The man on his side also reacted strangely. He said, "That's wonderful! We want you to excavate, and we'll furnish your permits, put you up in a place to stay and even pay for your meals!"

Ron did not know what to think – he knew it was a supernatural experience and it was the first of this kind despite having discovered by this time the remnants of Noah's Ark and the Chariots in the Red Sea. He had to decline the man's offer because he first wanted to research and study the Bible about the possible location of the Ark of the Covenant.

Ron found that the Ark disappeared from the divine record sometime between 621 BC and 586 BC. Since the temple in Jerusalem was completely destroyed, there was no doubt that the Ark was not there.

You can read in the Bible (2 Kings 24:13, 2 Kings 25:13-18 and Jeremiah 52:17-23) about all the valuable items, which were carried off to Babylon, even small spoons are mentioned but not the Ark.

Neither is it mentioned in the list of things brought back from Babylon in Ezra 1:7-1:11. Since we are told in Jeremiah 28:3 that everything taken to Babylon from the "House of the Lord" would be returned, we can deduce that the Ark was never taken to Babylon in the first place.

According to Ron's website he finally concluded:

1) The Ark had to have been hidden between the 18th year of Josiah, (when we are told
2) he had it taken to Solomon's temple), and 35 years later, when the temple was destroyed.

3) The Ark was not taken to Babylon, based on the information from the Scriptures.

4) The Ark was most likely hidden just prior to the destruction of the temple, when Jerusalem was surrounded by the Babylonian siege wall; and

5) The Ark was hidden somewhere within the confines of the city wall of Jerusalem and the Babylonian siege wall. The entire city and the temple were destroyed in 586 BC by the Babylonians, so the Ark could have only escaped destruction or captivity by not being anywhere in the city.

He decided to see if any mention was found in any non-Biblical records, especially Jewish. He found two intriguing instances. In the Apocryphal book of 2 Maccabees, we read:

2 Mac 2:2 The records show that it was Jeremiah who... 4,... prompted by a divine message, the prophet gave orders that the Tent of Meeting and the Ark should go with him. Then he went to the mountain from the top of which Moses saw God's promised land. 5 When he reached the mountain, Jeremiah found a cave dwelling; he carried the tent, the Ark, and the incense altar into it, then blocked up the entrance. 6 Some of his companions came to mark out the way, but were unable to find it. 7 When Jeremiah learned of this he reprimanded them. `The place shall remain unknown', he said, `until God finally gathers His people together and shows mercy to them. 8 Then the Lord will bring these things to light again, and the glory of the Lord will appear with the cloud, as it was seen both in the time of Moses, and when Solomon prayed that the shrine might be worthily consecrated.

So Ron concluded that the Ark was outside the ancient city wall and within the siege wall and he decided to go ahead with the excavation.

Ron and his team worked from 1979 – 1989, ten years. Did you ever work on a project for God with your own resources and money for ten years?

God did not make it easy.

They had scanning equipment to distinguish cracks or man made cavern activity; but it was complicated and perilous. (All footage on YouTube) When they climbed down the tunnel they got to a depth about 45 feet, because Jerusalem was destroyed ten times during antiquity and with each destruction new layers of rubble were created.

Up to eight men were laboring in a small square and hoisting up one bucket after another full of stone and debris to the surface. And for ten years Ron Wyatt never lost faith that since Babylonian times God had hidden this most holy relic under 50 feet of rubble.

One day Ron and his Arab companion were seeing a stalactite bigger than others. After having removed this stalactite they peeped into the cavity behind.

It was a chamber!

The Arab companion who was of a smaller size than Ron climbed into the hole and returned immediately, asking in a terrified voice: "What is in there?", then fleeing the site.

Ron crawled in and his eyes slowly distinguished stones and animal skins laden with dust and objects below like a golden table.

He could not see very well because the stones and debris were piled up high – but finally he discovered the Ark and saw a crack right above and a brown substance on the heavily dusted surface of the Ark.

Ron took a sample of this substance and brought it to a reliable laboratory in Jerusalem. They confirmed this substance to be blood, being alive and having one Y-chromosome and twenty-three X-chromosomes. We humans typically have 23 pairs of chromosomes, or 46 chromosomes in total. There is no recount of anyone having only one Y-chromosome. The one Y-Chromosome in this case must be from the father, God. Only he can create life in a different form. All facial features from his mother Mary's side were given with her twenty-three X-Chromosomes.

Ron visited this site five times by himself and at the last time it was cleared with every holy object on display in full splendor and two Angels telling him that the room would be sealed from now on. Ron was asked by the Angels to videotape the objects displayed and also the two tablets with the Ten Commandments – the tape was left in the chamber.

According to Ron Wyatt he was told that all would be revealed when the Mark-of-the-Beast-Law is passed or enforced. Ron said: 'If you keep the Ten Commandments, you will receive the Mark of God. Soon there will be a manmade law, which will enforce to break one of the Commandments, and then you receive the Mark of the Beast." God says about this 'Mark of the Beast":

Revelation13-18 (NIV)

He also forced everyone, small and great, rich and poor, free and slave, to receive a mark on his right hand or on his forehead, so that no one could buy or sell unless he had the mark, which is the name of the beast or the number of his name.

This calls for wisdom. If anyone has insight, let him calculate the number of the beast, for it is man's number. His number is 666.

Revelation is the most futuristic and scary book of the bible. These are the seven years where the wicked on earth are separated from the righteous. It will be a time of tribulation and a frightening era to live in but God can help us through it.

And at the end all remaining on earth will see this:

Revelation 11:19

Then God's temple in heaven was opened, and within his temple was seen the Ark of the Covenant. And there came flashes of lightning, rumblings, peals of thunder, an earthquake and a great hailstorm.

This is happening in the future when God's wrath of the wicked is completed after the seven-year tribulation. God will literally beam his holy treasure up into his heavenly temple – just like Star Wars movies. Then Jesus will start his reign of one millennium.

When does the tribulation start? One of the indications is the drying up of the Euphrates River. Research it, if you are interested. The river is drying up. Six hundred years before the crucifixion of his only son, God in his ingenuity placed his most holy object under the site of crucifixion. When Jesus was pierced in his side by the Roman Centurion the earth shook and cracked and down this crack the blood of Jesus dripped onto the mercy seat of the Ark of the Covenant, thus atoning for our sins. No one could have designed this better. Still, it is a sad thought to think a man unblemished had to suffer that pain for us.

Life is in the blood as the bible tells us.

Matthew 27:50-51 NIV

And when Jesus had cried out again in a loud voice, he gave up his spirit. At that moment the curtain of the temple was torn in half from top to bottom. The earth shook and the rocks split.

What Jesus felt when they crucified him:

Psalm 22:12-18 (KJV):

Many bulls have compassed me: strong bulls of Bashan have beset me round. They gaped upon me with their mouths, like a ravening and a roaring lion. I am poured out like water, and all my bones are out of joint: my heart is like wax; it is melted in the midst of my bowels. My strength is dried up like a potsherd; and my tongue cleaveth to my jaws; and thou hast brought me into the dust of death. For dogs have compassed me: the assembly of the wicked have inclosed me: they pierced my hands and my feet. I may tell all my bones: they look and stare upon me. They part my garments among them, and cast lots upon my vesture.

Evidence today

Ron Wyatt's personal recount on YouTube – listen to it and you should discern yourself if this man does speak the truth after having searched for ten years for the Ark.

According to Ron he also saw a man in ancient clothing when he was working at the site. This man talked to him and said: "God bless you and what you are doing here."

Testimony of Ian Thain, who was an eyewitness to a video shot inside the chamber of the Ark of the Covenant. Only a few saw the tape before Ron hid it again.

Ian Thain confirmed that he had seen many objects and supposedly the Ark, which was concealed even on the video with a light.

A cross-hole was found directly above the chamber of the Ark of the Covenant. Above the site of the crucifixion a metal detector was placed and it showed clear readings of metal below, probably the Ark of the Covenant with its gold content.

All in all this is inconclusive – unless you believe!

The Shroud of Turin

Did you ever wonder how Jesus' face looked?

Jesus lived – Paul and John wrote in their letters about Jesus, the miracles he performed, his sermons and parables, which are as valid today as they were yesterday. Jesus Christ gave up his life willingly to atone for our sins and transgressions. We only must believe in him and lead a life to please him and his Father.

When Jesus was tortured and maligned he could have put any of his adversaries to death in an instant. The accusers were the evil men and Jesus was without fault or sin - not fair by any means at all.

He knew beforehand who would betray him and what would happen to him. He prayed to God several times to take this cup away but only if his father wanted to take the cup away. And then Jesus went willingly not only as a sacrificial lamb but also to undergo malicious torture.

He did that for you and me so that we have eternal life in Heaven.

Meanwhile it is not always fair and easy living for those who believe because the devil reigns supreme in this world for the time being – until Jesus will return.

And we who believe in him can't wait for Jesus to appear gloriously in the sky. When Jesus died he was buried in the tomb of a rich man who also had clean new linen to wrap the body of Jesus for his burial.

Luke 23:50 NIV

Now there was a man named Joseph, a member of the Council, a good and upright man, who had not consented to their decision and action. He came from the Judean town of Arimathea and he was waiting for the kingdom of God. Going to Pilate, he asked for Jesus' body. Then he took it down, wrapped it in linen cloth and placed it in a tomb cut in the rock, one in which no one had yet been laid.....

Thieves and murderers who ended their lives on the cross did not have any rich friends who were buying expensive linen and donating their own burial chamber.

But this happened to Jesus.

God brought Jesus back to life on the third day and when this happened, God's energy, light or frequency was transferred onto the linen burial cloth and Jesus' face was imprinted as a negative image on this cloth. **This was a miracle!**

The linen wrapping was left in the burial chamber and had a long journey from Jerusalem to the Cathedral of St. John The Baptist in Turin, Italy, where it has been now for over four centuries.

Throughout history, the Shroud of Turin has been a source of deep spiritual significance. It has reinforced the faith of millions of Christians, brought a profound awareness of Christ's sufferings and inspired a response of love and devotion. Even today, the Shroud continues to be a tool for deepening understanding and appreciation of the sacrifice made by Jesus.

The Shroud stands apart from other relics due to its extensive scrutiny by scientists, historians, and theologians for over a century. Debates about its authenticity have been ongoing.

It has been tested and authenticated, then discredited for different reasons. This linen cloth features a distinctive herringbone pattern. Its dimensions are 436 cm In length and 110 cm in width, equivalent to about 14 feet 3 inches by 3 feet 7 inches.

An additional strip of linen, about 8 cm or 3 inches wide, is sewn along its length. This shroud is known for bearing the faint, brownish images of a man's front and back, resembling someone who has undergone crucifixion. The image is only present on one side of the cloth.

The density of the image varies, suggesting a correlation with the proximity of the body to the cloth when the image was formed. Notably, the shroud also exhibits carmine-colored stains, identified as bloodstains.

The Shroud is steeped in an ancient tradition that associates it with the burial cloth of Jesus Christ, as described in the Gospels. The correlation between the details on the Shroud and the biblical account of Jesus' passion is striking.

French historian Jean-Christian Petitfils has devoted over four decades to the study of the shroud and the evidence is compelling. The thorns are clearly imprinted on the cloth and there are traces of seeds, which are only found around Jerusalem. Jesus was flogged very violently with a Roman flagrum, which has two small balls and a barbell between them and the manifestation of this can be seen under a microscope.

A Roman soldier pierced Jesus into his side and one can see this penetration on the shroud.

The image on the shroud is verified and was embedded on the linen surface 2,000 years ago, based on age dating. Originally, the cloth was dated in 1988 using radiocarbon isotopic measurements and produced an erroneous date of 1260 to 1390 AD. Dr. Ray Rogers from Las Alamos Laboratories was able to show that the sample taken for Carbon-14 was not from the original cloth, but came from a heterogeneous sample that had been damaged by a fire and replaced centuries ago (there may have been fraud involved in the original age-date). The cloth has been dated by more than one method, with scientific procedures and it has become the most investigated artifact in history as scientists from all over the world try to figure out how a cloth could acquire a full-body image of a crucified body that is also a 360-degree image with holographic characteristics - in other words, it is way beyond our current technology.

It is the only image in history that has done so. The image is so clear, that God actually created a full-body statue of the crucified man, with all of his wounds.

Many other things have been found on the shroud including species of pollen (a large percentage are derived from Jerusalem, some flowers that only bloom in March and April in Jerusalem, grains of aragonite travertine that geochemically match the travertine at the site where Christ was crucified, and even possible Roman coin images over the eyes of the body that is now believed by some researchers to have been minted by Pontius Pilate).

And finally – when you look at this image, negative or otherwise, the face on the cloth imprinted is emanating such a peaceful and knowing countenance, just look at it and please feel Jesus's compassion for us all if you are searching for the truth. I never learnt about this at school – did you? If not, I wonder why….

This shroud had quite a journey through time and different locations.

Miraculously the shroud escaped destruction several times including two fires, the last one in 1997, when the Cathedral of Turin burnt down.

Mario Trematore, one of the firefighters on site, felt moved by a particular grace and an inner voice that told him 'Strike here, on this side, not here'. He took a sledgehammer and broke the glass protection where the shroud was positioned and he saved the relic.

He later said that if it had been the work of a great Italian Renaissance painter, he would not have taken that many risks.

According to Jean-Christian Petitfils there had to be a will of providence to preserve this shroud as a testimony to the world. Providence is the manifestation of God's will as a spiritual superpower – and all that God can establish.

The shroud and Jesus' face can readily be viewed on the net.

I cannot reproduce a better or more accurate image.

Look at it yourself and feel the serenity and peace emanating from this cloth – or what do you feel? The victim of the shroud was beaten to a bloody pulp and Satan doesn't want for you to have proof that Jesus existed and died an unimaginable death for us. And this is exactly why the enemy uses so many people to mock it and discount it. But scripture about Jesus' crucifixion describes the same horrible experience of the shroud victim and all of the above make it impossible to discount the burial cloth of Jesus.

Below an image of the thorny crown, which represents Christ's suffering for us but maybe also the road we have to travel to be close to Christ...And I believe he is coming soon.

In the clouds with a trumpet as the Bible says:

Revelation 1:7

Look, he is coming with the clouds, and every eye will see him, even those who pierced him; and all the peoples of the earth will mourn because of him. So shall it be! Amen.

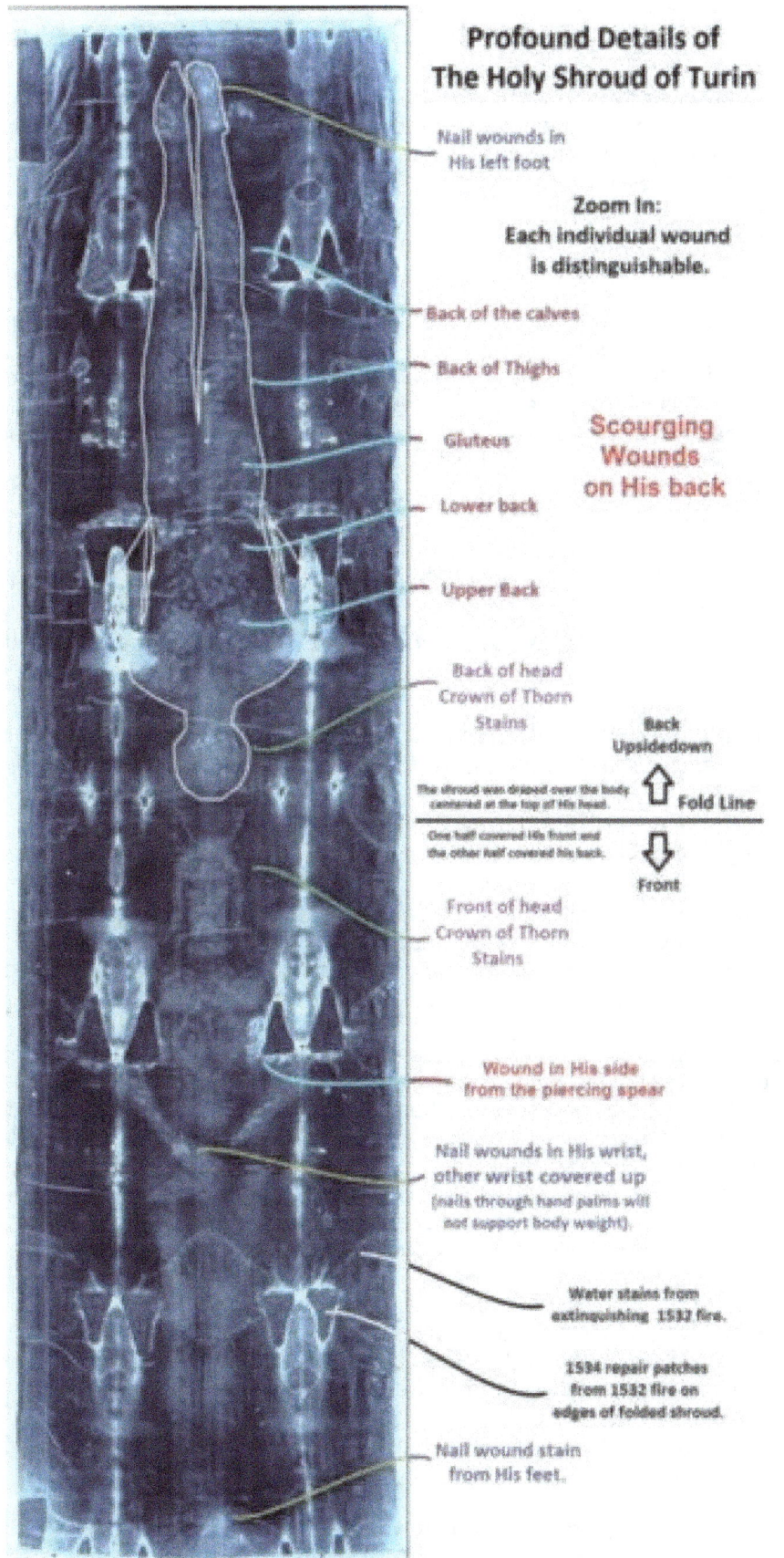

The Heart, Frequency and Emotions

The heart is the gateway between the soul and the spirit. Our soul (is actually a realm), which includes the mind, will, and emotions, is shaped by our thoughts and beliefs. The heart, or subconscious, holds the power to change our beliefs and ultimately shape our lives.

The Bible says, 'as a man thinks in his heart, so is he.' We have the ability to reprogram our hearts and experience a life filled with victory, fulfillment, joy, peace, and power, or walk in depression, poverty, wickedness, shame, and hopelessness.

Our hearts can also be broken and wounded, but the Lord is close to the brokenhearted and saves those who are crushed in spirit. The ultimate goal is to have love from a pure heart, with full assurance of faith, and a conscience that is free from evil. Remember, it is not just about what we do, but what is in our hearts that truly defines us. King David served as an inspiration as a man after God's heart. In Psalm 51, he acknowledged the importance of having a pure heart and continually seeking forgiveness from God. Let's follow in his footsteps and strive for a heart that is clean and focused on living a life that pleases the Lord.

Create in me a clean heart, O God, and renew a steadfast spirit within me - Psalm 51:10

Keep your heart with all diligence, for out of it spring the issues of life. - Proverbs 4:23

Now the purpose of the commandment is love from a pure heart, from a good conscience, and from sincere faith - 1 Timothy 1:5

Let us draw near with a true heart in full assurance of faith, having our hearts sprinkled from an evil conscience and our bodies washed with pure water - Hebrews 10:22

But he is a Jew who is one inwardly; and circumcision is that of the heart, in the Spirit, not in the letter; whose praise is not from men but from God. - Romans 2:29

Our heart energy comes from what is called the heart chakra located behind the heart organ. An open heart is giving. The more we give the more we receive, and it keeps building up to be bigger.

Our heart and our emotions are energy frequencies and their correlating sensations in our bodies are expansion or contraction. Feelings are the interpretations and labels we apply to the experience of emotion, such as sad, mad or glad.

David Hawkins, researcher and author of Power versus Force, demonstrates emotions as energy. He devised a scale that rates the energy level of basic human emotions with a range of 1 – 1,000. Anything below 200 is considered unhealthy for the individual; and society (shame 20, guilt 30, apathy 50, grief 75, fear 100, desire 125, anger 150, pride 175). All of the former God would like to eliminate!

Anything above 200 represents constructive expressions of power (courage 200, neutrality 250, willingness 310, acceptance 350, reason 400, love 500, joy 540, peace 600, enlightenment 700-1,000)

Every thought and emotion has its own vibrational frequency or wave frequency. That is why and how God can know our thoughts and how AI in the future with nanotechnology and graphene oxide will be able to manipulate mankind.

All materials emit a frequency and the bible tells us so......

According to new evidence by researcher Heidi Yellen, our human bodies have a frequency of 70 – 100m (in people with illness this drops below 50m). Dr. Yellen's premise was that any fabric with a higher frequency would be beneficial to us, and any fabric with a lower frequency causes or increases illness.

A nearly dead person has a frequency of 15. Materials like polyester, rayon and spandex register at a 15. Wool and linen do have a mega frequency of 5000, which energizes the body, and keeps it healthy. Linen also has anti-allergic properties.

However – you should not wear any garment woven of two different materials, in the case of linen and wool mixed together they cancel each other out and the beneficial properties have left entirely.

The Bible says:

"You shall not put on cloth from a mixture of two different materials"
(Leviticus 19:19 NIV)

So far we might have thought this is just another obligation to differentiate gentiles from Christians. No, it is a health recommendation by God.

Of course – if you do Hot yoga, wear the hot – yoga clothes for 90 minutes, wear your bike gear or fitness gear for the time you do the sport. Then switch over to healthy garments to support your own well-being.

The Pineal Gland or the Third Eye

Matthew 6:22-23 old Holy Bible by James McKay, Sydney 1879

The Light of the body is the eye: ***if therefore thine eye be single****, thy whole body shall be full of light. But if thine eye be evil, thy whole body shall be full of darkness. If therefore the light that is thee be darkness, how great is that darkness.*

To compare: Matthew 6:22-23 NIV

The eye is the lamp of the body. If your eyes are good, your whole body will be full of light. But if your eyes are bad, your whole body will be full of darkness. If then the light within you is darkness, how great is that darkness!

The last version is not quite as accurate as it refers to our two eyes. The lamp of our bodies is our Third Eye.

Jesus refers to our pineal gland, which is located below our brain. The third eye chakra or pineal gland is an energy center within the body on the forehead in the center of the brows. This eye is thought to help people become enlightened, spiritually awakened, or as the millennials say, "woke."

The pineal gland is a kind of atrophied photoreceptor, a light-sensing organ, an eye inside our brain which produces melatonin essential for a healthy sleep pattern.

Dr. Matthew Walker Ph.D. has done comprehensive studies on the pineal gland. He found that four different hormones are released every night, in wintertime between 10 pm and 3 am; therefore it is beneficial to go to bed early. These hormones are melatonin (The fix and rejuvenate hormone), Serotonin (the mood hormone), arginine-vasotocin (a natural painkiller) and epithalamion, which increases learning capacity.

God designed our brains to learn new things every day until we die. During our Non-REM sleep (rapid eye movement) waste and negative emotions are cleared away –

BUT ONLY AFTER WE FORGIVE!

God wants us to believe and forgive and has designed a natural boost system, which only works after we do as he asks us.

Rene Descartes, the French Philosopher living in the 1850s, believed the pineal gland to be our "principal seat of the soul". And as Jesus said, when the pineal gland becomes enlightened, then the whole body is full of light. This can only mean that we are walking a righteous path in the Light of God. In darkness there is no light and I wouldn't want to get lost in a soul of darkness, would you? It would be an unbearable sorrow.

In ideal circumstances we would want all of the chakras in our bodies to be aligned and properly energized, or?

One interesting fact: The pineal gland does calcify with Fluoride. Be careful of anything fluoridated.

And these are fifteen pineal gland decalcifiers: Mucuna, Reishi, Algae, Passionflower, Milk Thistle, Albizzia, Gingko, Blue Lotus, Gotu Kola, Noni, Shizandra, Moringa, Chaga, Aloe, Turmeric.

So how can we enlighten our pineal gland?

Through being calm, meditating, praying to God, searching for the divine truth.

Everyone living has to find out this truth for oneself, everyone is responsible for his own soul and must find out if there is an afterlife and therefore we must bear the consequences of what we believe and how we act here during our time on earth.

We are here on earth only a short time compared to eternity. Today we live a span of 60 to 90 years – what is that compared to eternity? As a Feng-Shui consultant I observed that change is frightening and often impossible for people.

The mind gradually adapts itself to the subjects upon which it is allowed to dwell. It is your choice at any time what to think, to speak, to do and change is important in life, not allowing change means avoiding progress.

Sylke Claridge

Wisdom

I sometimes hear from friends or relatives that they do not want to go down the rabbit hole. If knowledge is getting unpleasant or too difficult to comprehend or bear we often do not want to hear it.... What does God say about this?

Moral Benefits of Wisdom

Proverbs 2:1-15 NIV

*My son, if you accept my words
and store up my commands within you,
turning your ear to wisdom
and applying your heart to understanding—
indeed, if you call out for insight
and cry aloud for understanding,
and if you look for it as for silver
and search for it as for hidden treasure,
then you will understand the fear of the Lord
and find the knowledge of God.
For the Lord gives wisdom;
from his mouth come knowledge and understanding.
He holds success in store for the upright,
he is a shield to those whose walk is blameless,
for he guards the course of the just
and protects the way of his faithful ones.
Then you will understand what is right and just
and fair—every good path.
For wisdom will enter your heart,
and knowledge will be pleasant to your soul.
Discretion will protect you,
and understanding will guard you.
Wisdom will save you from the ways of wicked men,
from men whose words are perverse,
who have left the straight paths
to walk in dark ways,
who delight in doing wrong
and rejoice in the perverseness of evil,
whose paths are crooked
and who are devious in their ways.*

The Olive Tree

Romans 11:17

But if some of the branches were broken off, and you, being a wild olive, were grafted in among them and became partake with them of the rich root of the olive tree. Jeremiah 17:8 NIV

For he will be like a tree planted by the water, That extends its root by a stream And will not fear when the heat comes; But its leaves will be green, And it will not be anxious in a year of drought.
Nor cease to yield fruit.

God's Promise

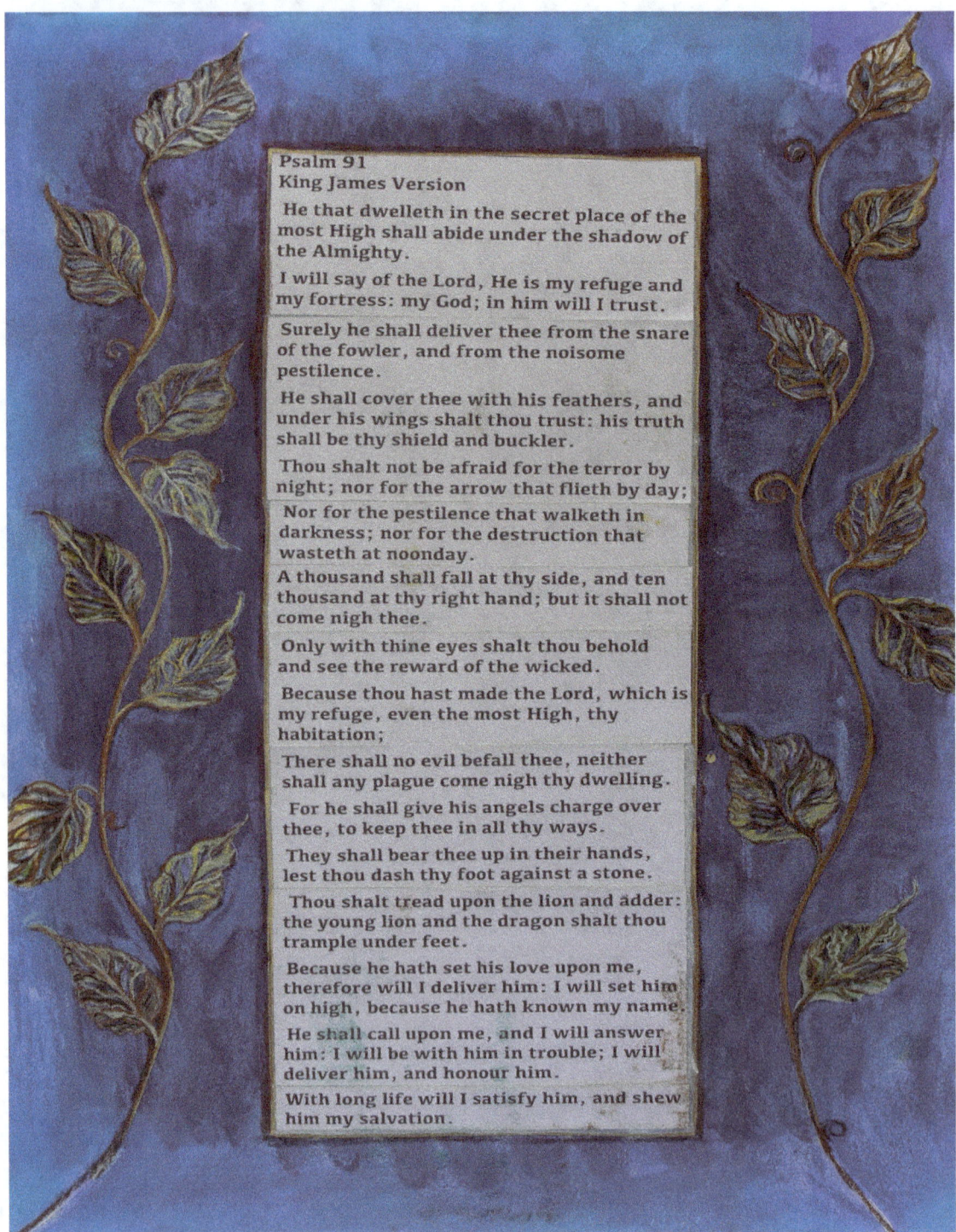

This is a very big promise and can only be kept by someone who has all the power of creation. No other can do that. Nature cannot do this. The Universe cannot do this for you. The stars cannot do this for you. They are all creations of God and Astrology is a valid science but you cannot rely on it for your salvation.

Miracles

Albert Einstein said "There are only two ways to live your life. One is as though nothing is a miracle. The other is as though everything is a miracle." I find this to be enchanting and life affirming – these three little sentences do lift my heart every time I read it. I always did and do believe in miracles but as a whole society we don't believe in miracles anymore because there is science?

And science can explain almost everything in its order, components, including miracles, supernatural events, or can science not?

And yet, there have been and there are miracles occurring which cannot be explained with any reasoning or science.

Once in a car on the Princes Highway here in Australia I heard a voice inside me – don't' ask where exactly – and I heard: "Shut the window immediately."

I followed through and wrenched the window up in an old Toyota. Instantaneously a big white bird flew straight into the window – we would surely have had an accident. Where did that voice come from, an Angel?

I believe so! I believed in God at that time.

And here are two testimonies of the power of God, of faith and prayer to God; the first happened during WWII at Okinawa in Japan, the second only recently during the atrocious bushfires on the South Coast of New South Wales in Australia, where lives and livestock and properties were lost and my neighbor Aaron, who knocked at my door at 5 am in the morning and told me where to go and kept me safe, had to shoot too many singed and staggering cows afflicted because the owners couldn't bear to terminate their own livestock.

Miracles of healing and rescue are a testimony that God is listening to our prayers today in the same fashion as from the beginning of creation.

The first story features Desmond Doss who was a Christian and also a conscientious objector of war, who nevertheless wanted to contribute as a citizen of the USA when he enlisted as a combat medic in the army during the Second World War.

During the bloody battle of Okinawa in Japan in May 1945 Desmond Doss spent twelve hours singlehandedly retrieving wounded soldiers, who were lowered off the cliff at Hacksaw Ridge into the arms of waiting soldiers.

Doss did not distinguish between American or Japanese soldiers and tried to rescue both.

In an interview with WFXR at the 75th anniversary of this rescue mission Desmond Doss Jr. related a few facts and said that hatred was groomed into the soldiers on both ends but his father was the exception.

"Here was one man, he was different. He didn't have hatred."

God doesn't want us to hate even our enemies, we shall love everyone as also Jesus remarked in Luke 6:27-38 KJV (King James Version)

"But I say to you which hear, Love your enemies, do good to them which hate you, bless them that curse you, and pray for them which despitefully use you."

Very difficult to put into practice even without risking your life. Desmond Doss did it.

Desmond Doss saved at least 75 soldiers that night. To go back again and again onto the battlefield and search for soldiers still breathing whilst under sniper fire is on view in Mel Gibson's masterly done movie 'Hacksaw Ridge'. Please watch the movie if you can find it.

Doss had no companion to help him and still he had no fear or did it anyway because he was fueled and compelled again and again by an internal force – and that is how God works in us when we believe.

The other miracle happened to a good friend of mine, Dave Jeffery, and this is his story with his own words, also featured on numerous TV stations worldwide at the time:

As news of the approaching fire reached Mallacoota in the early hours of New Year's Eve, Jeffery and his neighbors were preparing to defend their homes against "an ember attack".

This ember attack quickly turned into a firewall and an estimated 2,000 residents and tourists were huddled together at the beach, ready to jump into the water, which would have been perilous as the air was sucked out above.

As the firewall loomed – which Jeffery says was reported to be 60 feet high and moving at 90 kilometers an hour – Jeffery and two older "prayer warriors" were praying.

"We could hear the roar. It sounded like a thousand freight trains coming at us. Then a huge gust, like someone had opened the door of a furnace, pushed us … It went black as black. The smoke was so thick it was hard to breathe."

"I prayed, 'Lord if you don't push this fire back now, we need wind from the east.'" No easterly was forecast at the time….

" As soon as I said that it started blowing from the east a little bit. Then I got louder and the wind got stronger. Then I got louder again and it got stronger again …

"I felt it change. I noticed that the bolder I got, the stronger the wind got. I was yelling 'In Jesus' name, thank you Lord for rescuing these souls. Push it back Lord, rescue us!'

"It was desperation personified. I did not care who heard me. I knew then that God was then doing what I was asking. Because if he didn't answer then, we were dead."

"What God did was push the fire back from the east, which was impossible but he did it. He did that for five minutes, which broke the fire front enough to stop it from getting to where we were."

"This was so impossible, but somehow God turned off the flames, like flicking off a switch." –

"My neighbors – who are not Christians – were eyewitnesses and they tell me 'God saved us'.

"They've seen a miracle. They've seen the supernatural – flames getting pushed back, they've seen the embers hit the grass and not burn, without even a single mark."

And David Jeffery's final words: "It's time for people to rise up and pray. It's time to get serious about God and get back into reading his word."

How do you pray?

Luke 11:1-4

One day Jesus was praying in a certain place. When he finished, one of his disciples said to him, "Lord, teach us to pray, just as John taught his disciples."

He said to them, "When you pray, say:

"Father, hallowed be your name.
your kingdom come.
Give us each our daily bread.
Forgive us our sins,
For we also forgive everyone who has sinned against us.
And lead us not into temptation.

Jesus also said in Mark 11.24 NIV

"Therefore I say to you: What things soever you desire when you pray, believe that you receive them, and you shall have them."

So when we pray, we could have a miracle happen in our lives! God wants us I believe to pray with our hearts, full throttle, with full engagement, profoundly. He says is Jeremiah 29:13 NIV

"You will seek me and find me when you seek me with all your heart."

We all here on earth are fashioned with a heart. Our hearts have a frequency and ability to reach God and be heard by him, I call this miraculous in itself. Please have a try! With a heartfelt prayer, with sincerity and persistence you will be brought into God's awareness and presence so that the Holy Spirit can work on and with you and God will release his grace into your life and the lives you are praying for.

Jesus had something to say about a faithful prayer as well in Matthew 17.20-21 NIV:

"I tell you the truth, if you have faith as small as a mustard seed, you can say to this mountain, 'Move from here to there' and it will move. Nothing will be impossible for you."

Mustard seeds are minuscule....

God knows our Thoughts.

Psalms 139:1-6 (NIV)

You have searched me, LORD, and you know me. You know when I sit and when I rise; you perceive my thoughts from afar. You discern my going out and my lying down; you are familiar with all my ways. Before a word is on my tongue you, LORD, know it completely.

Fifteen hundred years after Noah's great flood, King Solomon was receiving some advice from his father, King David, who said this, " *... for the Lord searches all hearts, and understands every intent of the thoughts"* 1 Chronicles 28:9. In other words,

"Be aware of what's in your head, son. God sees it."

Today science has discovered that with our thoughts we send light & frequency into the atmosphere. This light of thought emanates from your mind and connects with the universal consciousness aka God. He can read our mind and knows our thoughts. If the pineal gland, the bridge between realms, is enlightened, communication with God might be more easily facilitated.

As God knows our thoughts you can experiment with water to contain your thoughts, frequency and emotion!

When you talk to a petri dish of water with love and then freeze this lovingly spoken to water the result is stunning with beautifully formed ice crystals. On the contrary when you express your distaste or hate to the water it will form crystals, which are jarred and rugged, and not pleasing to the eye. This discovery has been made by Dr. Masaro Emoto who has photographed thousands of water crystals throughout his years of research. The most beautiful and life affirming crystal response was when the water was told these words:

"Love and gratitude".

Look at the world we are living in. Are we living in a world full of love and gratitude? – Unfortunately it is not so. I would rather live in a world where love is reigning, justice, ethics and adherence to the word of God.

CONCLUSION

What is the undeniably truth of these miracles if you search your heart – what cannot be denied?

Which signs or miracles you have on these pages are indisputable, undeniable, and

uncontestable?

- The survival of eight people and all animals on an Ark and a big flood wiping out all mankind who didn't make it into the Ark?
- Ron Wyatt has found Noah's Ark and all evidence is there.

- Destruction of Sodom and Gomorrah because not even ten upright people could be found?

The cities are still standing today with evidence of burnt and still intact sulfur balls of purity not found anywhere else on this earth.

- The safe passage through the Red Sea when one million Israelites were pursued by a Pharaoh with a mighty army.

Ron Wyatt has found the site and several divers have taken sufficient photos and videos.

- Water flowing out of a rock for one million Israelites and their livestock?

The Split Rock of Rephidim has clear signs of water erosion and looks like being split in half!

- God descending on a mountain?

Mount Horeb is the mountain. No other peak has the geological formation of a black crust only having penetrated the outer surface of all stones.

- Jesus lived and died for our sins.
- The Shroud of Turin has evidence of facial features, blood, thorns and there is no other linen cloth of that age which has any of these signs or features embedded.

Now it is your call. What do you think in your heart? What are your actions from now on?

Do you believe that these miracles happened? Wouldn't it be lovely when we all meet each other in Heaven? People with a good heart, even those who have sinned but repented and have been forgiven.

How long do you have time to decide? Cut-off time is your death. Do you know when you will die?

Eschatology

Eschatology is the part of Theology concerned with death, judgement, and the final destiny of our soul and of humankind.

Christian hope is concerned with eschatology, or the science of last things.

As much as you can read and study the bible, there are always contradictions and only the Holy Spirit can truly reveal things to come.

Revelation tells us of the Seven-year tribulation where Christians will be persecuted again.

But when it is exactly is difficult to predict.

One hint is given in Daniel 9.25 KJV

25 Know therefore and understand, that from the going forth of the commandment to restore and to build Jerusalem unto the Messiah the Prince shall be seven weeks, and threescore and two weeks: the street shall be built again, and the wall, even in troublous times. (here every week signifies one year = 483 years)

26 And after threescore and two weeks shall Messiah be cut off, but not for himself: and the people of the prince that shall come shall destroy the city and the sanctuary; and the end thereof shall be with a flood, and unto the end of the war desolations are determined.

27 And he shall confirm the covenant with many for one week: and in the midst of the week he shall cause the sacrifice and the oblation to cease, and for the overspreading of abominations he shall make it desolate, even until the consummation, and that determined shall be poured upon the desolate. (this refers to the seven-year tribulation)

The Antichrist is to come sometime in the near future. His reign is seven years and in the middle of his power he will install the Abomination of desolation, something very revolting to God. He will also demand as mentioned beforehand for everyone to receive a mark on their foreheads or hands and without this mark one cannot buy or sell. Troubled times.

An indication where this is fitting in:

…. Around 1535, when Jerusalem was part of the Ottoman Empire, Sultan Suleiman I ordered the ruined City walls of Jerusalem to be rebuilt. The work took around four years from 1537 to 1541.

The Bible says that 'from going forth of the commandment to restore and build Jerusalem unto the Messiah the Prince (here- The Antichrist) it will be 483 years.

Add 483 + 1535 + 2018.

A year according to God at the time of Daniel's prophecy consisted of thirteen months and exactly 364 days. In 46 BC, the Roman ruler Julius Caesar established the Julian calendar, which was built solely on the solar year.

From that time each year consisted of 365 days plus one day in every fourth year.

Mathematical conclusion: Since 46 BC each year consists of 1.25 days more than before that time.

46 + 2024= 2070 with 1.25 days too many. Multiply 2070 x 1.25 and then divide by 364 = 7.1

This means we must add 7 years to 2018 = 2025 - and maybe, if this is the right interpretation, this could be the year the Antichrist will be arriving.

First, he brings peace and we might be confounded, after 3.5 years the situation will change and we must hold strongly onto our faith.

And the last bit: Why the Bible is important today.

Yes, this book is ancient. And it is not an easy task to read it. But when you start and believe that these stories are true, it is riveting. And you'll find passages referring to your current situation. Especially if you pray and ask and then get an answer in your mind which Psalm or Bible passage to read – this is one way God can help us to navigate our problems and difficult situations.

You know when you please God, as there will be a light switched on inside you. The new slogan today is 'We are hackable animals' and there is no God in the sky. AI is advertised as the ultimate existence and we are invited to join in with our bodies. But there is a God as you can see today by his miracle-remnants. Under him exists the devil, the Kingdom of Heaven & Earth with us people having one precious lifetime to figure out the truth and then walk in the way of our creator.

Please open your heart and ask yourself if this could be true? The devil who reigns in this world, tries everything and anything to deceive you and distract you. How much time are we spending in front of a black box or on our phones?

Take a tenth of that time and figure out what is really happening around you.

What is worthy of your pursuit of living decently?

Short-lived pleasures, video games and distraction?

Or looking for the one who promises you an eternal belonging to a just God?

The ultimate question is:

How much effort would you want to put into your destiny when you perceive the reality of a life after death? The supernatural is real and there is a Heaven and Hell.

The littlest of effort?

An effort?

A mighty effort?

The biggest effort for the rest of your life?

'Living is not enough. One must fight and protect what is precious'
(loosely based on the movie 'The Ramen Shop')

May God bless you all and keep you safe!

Bibliography & other Sources

- The Bible, NIV and KJV
- The Book of Enoch, Complete Edition, translated by R.H. Charles (IAP 2009)
- Missing Books of the Bible, Immanuel Shaddai Fellowship
- The Dead Sea Scrolls uncovered by R. Eisenman & M. Wise
- The Book of Jasher – Audiobooks read by Christopher Glyn
- Rob Skiba – The Archeon Invasion
- Rob Skiba – The Genesis Revelation – Declaring the End from the Beginning
- Sodom and Gomorrah : The Cities of the Plain with Photos by Kevin Fisher https://nebula.wsimg.com/cb77af291104b4e6267e93c0894c5ae7?AccessKeyId=1C7E0DBE4EB9AEE100A8&disposition=0&alloworigin=1
- Michael Heizer
- Timothy Alberino 'Birthright'
- Isaiah Saldivar
- Steve Quayle – Vimeo.com Channel GenSix
- Chuck Missler Ten Part Series on Genesis
- HolyLandSite.com
- Ron Wyatt Foundation
- The Split Rock and Battlefield at Rephidim by Doubting Thomas Research Foundation https://doubtingthomasresearch.com/split-rock-battlefield-rephidim/
- The Split Rock of Rephidim http://www.truth-absolute.com/found--split-rock.html
- Split Rock of Rephidim https://visitmountsinaiarabia.com
- The Shroud of Turin https://www.ncregister.com/interview/holy-shroud-of-turin-s-authenticity-can-no-longer-be-disputed-expert-asserts
- - https://shroud.com,
- https://www.shroudcenter.com
- https://www.shroudofturin.com
- The Shroud of Turin – Website of the National Catholic Register
- Timo Bhely created a good video of his visit to Mount Horeb (YouTube)
- 'The Untold Story of Fluoridation: Revisiting the Changing Perspectives' by the Indian Journal of Occupational and Environmental Medicine
- David R. Hawkins M.D. Ph.D. , 'Power versus Force'

www.ingramcontent.com/pod-product-compliance
Lightning Source LLC
Chambersburg PA
CBHW080325080526
44585CB00021B/2481